Kaplan Publishing are constantly fi [ways] to make a difference to your studies and our exciting online resources really do offer something different to students looking for exam success.

KT-232-419

This book comes with free MyKaplan online resources so that you can study anytime, anywhere. **This free online resource is not sold separately and is included in the price of the book.**

Having purchased this book, you have access to the following online study materials:

CONTENT	AAT	
	Text	Kit
Electronic version of the book	✓	✓
Progress tests with instant answers	✓	
Mock assessments online	✓	✓
Material updates	✓	✓

How to access your online resources

Kaplan Financial students will already have a MyKaplan account and these extra resources will be available to you online. You do not need to register again, as this process was completed when you enrolled. If you are having problems accessing online materials, please ask your course administrator.

If you are not studying with Kaplan and did not purchase your book via a Kaplan website, to unlock your extra online resources please go to www.mykaplan.co.uk/addabook (even if you have set up an account and registered books previously). You will then need to enter the ISBN number (on the title page and back cover) and the unique pass key number contained in the scratch panel below to gain access. You will also be required to enter additional information during this process to set up or confirm your account details.

If you purchased through Kaplan Flexible Learning or via the Kaplan Publishing website you will automatically receive an e-mail invitation to MyKaplan. Please register your details using this email to gain access to your content. If you do not receive the e-mail or book content, please contact Kaplan Publishing.

Your Code and Information

This code can only be used once for the registration of one book online. This registration and your online content will expire when the final sittings for the examinations covered by this book have taken place. Please allow one hour from the time you submit your book details for us to process your request.

Please scratch the film to access your MyKaplan code.

Please be aware that this code is case-sensitive and you will need to include the dashes within the passcode, but not when entering the ISBN. For further technical support, please visit www.MyKaplan.co.uk

AAT

AQ2016

Management Accounting: Budgeting

EXAM KIT

This Exam Kit supports study for the following AAT qualifications:
AAT Professional Diploma in Accounting – Level 4
AAT Level 4 Diploma in Business Skills
AAT Professional Diploma in Accounting at SCQF Level 8

British Library Cataloguing-in-Publication Data

A catalogue record for this book is available from the British Library.

Published by:

Kaplan Publishing UK

Unit 2 The Business Centre

Molly Millar's Lane

Wokingham

Berkshire

RG41 2QZ

ISBN: 978-1-78740-533-2

© Kaplan Financial Limited, 2019

Printed and bound in Great Britain.

CONTENTS

Features in this exam kit

In addition to providing a wide ranging bank of real exam style questions, we have also included in this kit:

- unit-specific information and advice on exam technique

- our recommended approach to make your revision for this particular unit as effective as possible.

You will find a wealth of other resources to help you with your studies on the AAT website:

www.aat.org.uk/

Quality and accuracy are of the utmost importance to us so if you spot an error in any of our products, please send an email to mykaplanreporting@kaplan.com with full details, or follow the link to the feedback form in MyKaplan.

Our Quality Co-ordinator will work with our technical team to verify the error and take action to ensure it is corrected in future editions.

UNIT-SPECIFIC INFORMATION

THE EXAM

FORMAT OF THE ASSESSMENT

The assessment will comprise eight independent tasks. Students will be assessed by computer-based assessment.

In any one assessment, students may not be assessed on all content, or on the full depth or breadth of a piece of content. The content assessed may change over time to ensure validity of assessment, but all assessment criteria will be tested over time.

The learning outcomes for this unit are as follows:

	Learning outcome	Weighting
1	Prepare forecasts of income and expenditure	10%
2	Prepare budgets	35%
3	Demonstrate how budgeting can improve organisational performance	35%
4	Report budgetary information to management in a clear and appropriate format	20%
	Total	100%

Time allowed

2 hours 30 minutes

PASS MARK

The pass mark for all AAT CBAs is 70%.

 Always keep your eye on the clock and make sure you attempt all questions!

DETAILED SYLLABUS

The detailed syllabus and study guide written by the AAT can be found at:

www.aat.org.uk/

INDEX TO QUESTIONS AND ANSWERS

KAPLAN PUBLISHING

EXAM TECHNIQUE

- **Do not skip any of the material** in the syllabus.

- **Read each question** *very* carefully.

- **Double-check your answer** before committing yourself to it.

- Answer **every** question – if you do not know an answer to a multiple choice question or true/false question, you don't lose anything by guessing. Think carefully before you **guess**.

- If you are answering a multiple-choice question, **eliminate first those answers that you know are wrong**. Then choose the most appropriate answer from those that are left.

- **Don't panic** if you realise you've answered a question incorrectly. Getting one question wrong will not mean the difference between passing and failing.

Computer-based exams – tips

- Do not attempt a CBA until you have **completed all study material** relating to it.

- On the AAT website there is a CBA demonstration. It is **ESSENTIAL** that you attempt this before your real CBA. You will become familiar with how to move around the CBA screens and the way that questions are formatted, increasing your confidence and speed in the actual exam.

- Be sure you understand how to use the **software** before you start the exam. If in doubt, ask the assessment centre staff to explain it to you.

- Questions are **displayed on the screen** and answers are entered using keyboard and mouse. At the end of the exam, you are given a certificate showing the result you have achieved.

- In addition to the traditional multiple-choice question type, CBAs will also contain **other types of questions**, such as number entry questions, drag and drop, true/false, pick lists or drop down menus or hybrids of these.

- In some CBAs you will have to type in complete computations or written answers.

- You need to be sure you **know how to answer questions** of this type before you sit the exam, through practice.

KAPLAN'S RECOMMENDED REVISION APPROACH

QUESTION PRACTICE IS THE KEY TO SUCCESS

Success in professional examinations relies upon you acquiring a firm grasp of the required knowledge at the tuition phase. In order to be able to do the questions, knowledge is essential.

However, the difference between success and failure often hinges on your exam technique on the day and making the most of the revision phase of your studies.

The **Kaplan Study Text** is the starting point, designed to provide the underpinning knowledge to tackle all questions. However, in the revision phase, poring over text books is not the answer.

Kaplan Pocket Notes are designed to help you quickly revise a topic area; however you then need to practise questions. There is a need to progress to exam style questions as soon as possible, and to tie your exam technique and technical knowledge together.

The importance of question practice cannot be over-emphasised.

The recommended approach below is designed by expert tutors in the field, in conjunction with their knowledge of the examiner and the specimen assessment.

You need to practise as many questions as possible in the time you have left.

OUR AIM

Our aim is to get you to the stage where you can attempt exam questions confidently, to time, in a closed book environment, with no supplementary help (i.e. to simulate the real examination experience).

Practising your exam technique is also vitally important for you to assess your progress and identify areas of weakness that may need more attention in the final run up to the examination.

In order to achieve this we recognise that initially you may feel the need to practice some questions with open book help.

Good exam technique is vital.

KAPLAN PUBLISHING

THE KAPLAN REVISION PLAN

Stage 1: Assess areas of strengths and weaknesses

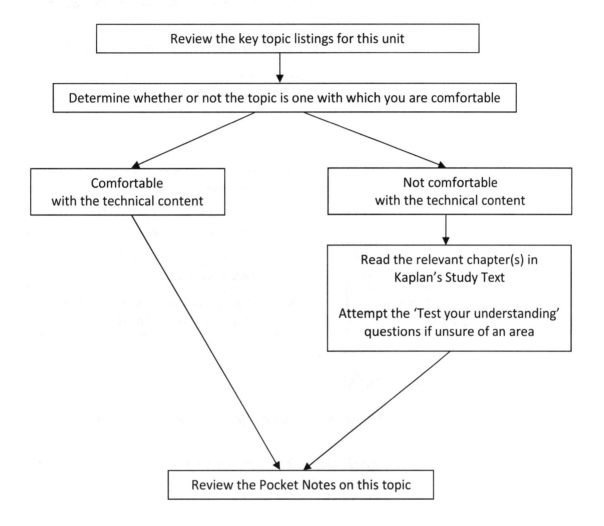

Stage 2: Practice questions

Follow the order of revision of topics as presented in this Kit and attempt the questions in the order suggested.

Try to avoid referring to Study Texts and your notes and the model answer until you have completed your attempt.

Review your attempt with the model answer and assess how much of the answer you achieved.

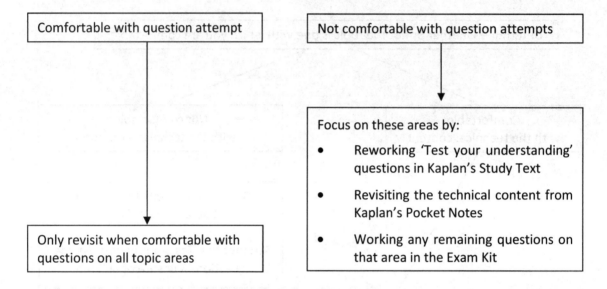

Stage 3: Final pre-exam revision

We recommend that you **attempt at least one mock examination** containing a set of previously unseen exam-standard questions.

Attempt the mock CBA online in timed, closed book conditions to simulate the real exam experience.

Section 1

PRACTICE QUESTIONS

SOURCES OF INFORMATION

1   SOURCES (I)

Match each item of budget data below with its appropriate source.

Data	Source
UK interest rates	SWOT analysis
Competitor prices	European Union
UK economic growth forecasts	Pricing research
	UK Treasury, independent economics consultants
	Bank of England
	Sydney Morning Herald

2   SOURCES (II)

Match each item of budget data below with its appropriate source.

Data	Source
UK tax rates	Internal analysis
UK house prices	European Union
Customer tastes	Market research
	HMRC publications
	Foreign office
	Building society data

3   SOURCES (III)

Match each item of budget data below with its appropriate source.

Data	Source
French tax rates	Building Society data
Political party likely to win power	Market research
Customer preferences	Opinion poll surveys
	HMRC publications
	French government
	New Delhi Times

4   SOURCES (IV)

Match each item of budget data below with its appropriate source.

Data	Source
UK economic growth forecasts	Brazilian government
UK duty rates (tax on alcohol etc.)	New York Times
Brazilian import tax rates	Market research
	HMRC publications
	UK Treasury, independent economics consultants
	Sydney morning herald

BUDGETARY RESPONSIBILITIES

5   CONTACTS (I)

Match each task with the individual or group that you will need to contact for information.

Situation	Contact
You want to identify any production constraints	Trade union representative
You want to forecast the cost of labour	Board of Directors
The budget is ready for final approval	Suppliers
	Budget committee
	Production planning manager

6   CONTACTS (II)

Match each task with the individual or group that you will need to contact for information.

Situation	Contact
You want to know the future strategy of the firm	Pressure group
You want to forecast the cost of machinery	Board of directors
You want to assess the efficiency of labour	Buyer
	Machinery buyers
	Management accountants

7   CONTACTS (III)

Match each task with the individual or group that you will need to contact for information.

Situation	Contact
You want to know day to day regional firm policy	Machine operator
You want to forecast sales	Board of directors
You want to know idle time last period	Regional manager
	Management accountants
	Sales team

8   CONTACTS (IV)

Match each task with the individual or group that you will need to contact for information.

Situation	Contact
You want to forecast the price of raw materials	Managing director
You want to examine competitors' prices	Suppliers
You want to check the availability of skilled labour	Other firms' price lists
	Firms' buying department
	Employment agency

9 THE RIGHT BUDGET

Drag each item of revenue or cost in the list below and drop it into its appropriate budget.

Cost
New machinery
Salary of HR Manager
Magazine advertising
New delivery van
Raw material usage
Incentives paid to sales staff
Spare parts for production machines
Salaries of repair engineers
Wages of assembly line workers

Capital expenditure	Marketing

Personnel	Cost of production

Maintenance

10 CUMIN COMPANY

The Cumin Company expects to produce 10,000 units in the month of December. Each unit requires 0.5 kgs of material X. During the production process 2% of material X is wasted. The business will start December with 900 kgs of X and will end the month with 950 kgs. Material X costs £1 per kg.

Complete the following resource budget for materials:

Resource Budget – Material X	Units	December
Needed for production		
Wastage		
Total requirement		
Closing inventory		
Opening Inventory		
Purchases in month		
Cost per kg		
Purchase cost of Material X		

11   DRAG AND DROP

Drag each item of revenue or cost in the list below and drop it into its appropriate budget.

Cost	Capital expenditure	Marketing
Television advertising		
Enhancements to production machines		
Wages of IT engineers		
Wages of production line workers	Personnel	Cost of production
New conveyor belt		
Salary of IT Manager		
Commissions paid to sales staff		
Salary of HR Manager		

IT

12   ADAM

Drag each item of revenue or cost in the list below and drop it into its appropriate budget.

Cost	Capital expenditure	Marketing
New photocopier		
Salary of HR Manager		
Radio advertising		
Raw material usage		
Spare parts for production machines	Personnel	Cost of production
Cost of machinery repairs		
Lighting costs for factory		
Market research costs		
New cars		
Cost of HR staff		
New building	Maintenance	
Cost of heating factory		
Bonuses paid to sales team		
Internet advertising		
Spare parts for old trucks		
Wages of assembly line workers		

ACCOUNTING TREATMENT OF OVERHEADS

13   ACCOUNTING TREATMENT (I)

Select the most appropriate accounting treatment for each of the following costs.

- Materials used in the production process
- Administrative wages
- Depreciation of production equipment
- Advertising costs
- Rent of the labour intensive production facility
- Office stationery
- Idle time pay for production workers
- Overtime Premium for production workers

Options available in drop down boxes against each item are:

- Allocate to marketing overheads
- Allocate to administrative overheads
- Direct cost
- Charge to production in a machine hour overhead rate
- Charge to production in a labour hour overhead rate

14   ACCOUNTING TREATMENT (II)

Select the most appropriate accounting treatment for each of the following costs.

- Materials used in the production process
- Rent of a machine intensive production facility
- Office paper
- Basic pay for production workers
- Secretarial wages
- Overtime premium for production workers
- Payments to marketing staff

Options available in drop down boxes against each item are:

- Allocate to marketing overheads
- Allocate to administrative overheads
- Direct cost
- Charge to production in a machine hour overhead rate
- Charge to production in a labour hour overhead rate

15   ACCOUNTING TREATMENT (III)

Select the most appropriate accounting treatment for each of the following costs.

- Wood used in the production process
- General postage costs
- Internet advertising costs
- Office stationery
- Chemicals used in the production process
- Idle time pay for production workers
- Power costs for machinery

Options available in drop down boxes against each item are:

- Allocate to marketing overheads
- Allocate to administrative overheads
- Direct cost
- Charge to production in a machine hour overhead rate
- Charge to production in a labour hour overhead rate

INDICES

16   TACO

The budget committee has set the sales volume growth and pricing assumptions for years 2, 3 4 and 5 in the form of indices.

Complete the sales revenue forecast below. Do not show decimals. Round each figure to the nearest whole number.

	Year 1	Year 2	Year 3	Year 4	Year 5
Sales volume index	100	102	107	107	108
Sales price index	110	111	112	113	115

Sales revenue	Actual Year 1 £	Forecast Year 2 £	Forecast Year 3 £	Forecast Year 4 £	Forecast Year 5 £
At Year 1 prices	120,000				
At expected prices					

17   ARCHER

The budget committee has set the sales volume growth and pricing assumptions for years 2, 3 4 and 5 in the form of indices.

Complete the sales revenue forecast below. Do not show decimals. Round each figure to the nearest whole number.

	Year 1	Year 2	Year 3	Year 4	Year 5
Sales volume index	120	121	122	123	124
Sales price index	112	115	120	125	130

Sales revenue	Actual Year 1 £	Forecast Year 2 £	Forecast Year 3 £	Forecast Year 4 £	Forecast Year 5 £
At Year 1 prices	275,000				
At expected prices					

18   FLASH

The budget committee has set the sales volume growth and pricing assumptions for years 2, 3 4 and 5 in the form of indices.

Complete the sales revenue forecast below. Do not show decimals. Round each figure to the nearest whole number.

	Year 1	Year 2	Year 3	Year 4	Year 5
Sales volume index	118	121	122	123	124
Sales price index	112	115	120	125	130

Sales revenue	Actual Year 1 £	Forecast Year 2 £	Forecast Year 3 £	Forecast Year 4 £	Forecast Year 5 £
At Year 1 prices	280,000				
At expected prices					

19 SOPHIE

The budget committee has set the sales volume growth and pricing assumptions for years 2, 3 4 and 5 in the form of indices.

Complete the sales revenue forecast below. Do not show decimals. Round each figure to the nearest whole number.

	Year 1	Year 2	Year 3	Year 4	Year 5
Sales volume index	118	120	125	127	128
Sales price index	112	115	120	125	130

Sales revenue	Actual Year 1 £	Forecast Year 2 £	Forecast Year 3 £	Forecast Year 4 £	Forecast Year 5 £
At Year 1 prices	280,000				
At expected prices					

PRODUCTION BUDGETS

20 TITANIA

Complete the following production forecast for product 'Titania'. Round any decimal figures up to the next whole number of units, if necessary.

Closing inventory should be 30% of the following week's sales volume. 3% of all production fails quality controls checks and is rejected.

Production (units)	Week 1	Week 2	Week 3	Week 4	Week 5
Opening inventory	20,000				
Good production					
Sales Volume	65,000	66,000	67,000	70,000	72,000
Closing inventory					

Rejected Production				
Total manufactured units				

21 PUCK

Complete the following production forecast for product 'Puck'. **Round any decimal figures up to the next whole number of units, if necessary.**

Closing inventory should be 30% of the following week's sales volume. 4% of all production fails quality controls checks and is rejected.

Production (units)	Week 1	Week 2	Week 3	Week 4	Week 5
Opening inventory	35,000				
Good production					
Sales Volume	80,000	78,000	78,000	70,000	80,000
Closing inventory					

Rejected Production					
Total manufactured units					

22 OBERON

Complete the following production forecast for product 'Oberon'. **Round any decimal figures up to the next whole number of units, if necessary.**

Closing inventory should be 30% of the following week's sales volume. 10% of all production fails quality controls checks and is rejected.

Production (units)	Week 1	Week 2	Week 3	Week 4	Week 5
Opening inventory	32,000				
Good production					
Sales Volume	78,000	78,000	75,000	70,000	80,000
Closing inventory					

Rejected Production					
Total manufactured units					

23 LYSANDER

Complete the following production forecast for product 'Lysander'. **Round any decimal figures up to the next whole number of units, if necessary.**

Closing inventory should be 30% of the following week's sales volume. 2% of all production fails quality controls checks and is rejected.

Production (units)	Week 1	Week 2	Week 3	Week 4	Week 5
Opening inventory	20,000				
Good production					
Sales Volume	65,000	65,000	67,000	70,000	72,000
Closing inventory					

Rejected Production					
Total manufactured units					

24   DEMETRIUS

Complete the following production forecast for product 'Demetrius'. Round any decimal figures up to the next whole number of units, if necessary.

Closing inventory should be 30% of the following week's sales volume. 2% of all production fails quality controls checks and is rejected.

Production (units)	Week 1	Week 2	Week 3	Week 4	Week 5
Opening inventory	19,000				
Good production					
Sales Volume	65,000	66,000	67,000	70,000	72,000
Closing inventory					

Rejected Production				
Total manufactured units				

25   HERMIA

Complete the following production forecast for product 'Hermia'. Round any decimal figures up to the next whole number of units, if necessary.

Closing inventory should be 30% of the following week's sales volume. 3% of all production fails quality controls checks and is rejected.

Production (units)	Week 1	Week 2	Week 3	Week 4	Week 5
Opening inventory	19,000				
Good production					
Sales Volume	65,000	66,000	67,000	70,000	80,000
Closing inventory					

Rejected Production				
Total manufactured units				

26   EVIE

Complete the following production forecast for product A.

Units of product A	Week 1	Week 2	Week 3	Week 4	Week 5
Opening inventory	1,000				
Production					
Sub-total					
Sales	7,000	8,000	7,500	7,000	8,000
Closing inventory					

Closing inventory should be 25% of the following week's forecast sales.

(All gaps are numeric.)

27 EGO

Complete the following production forecast for the 'Ego'.

Units of Ego	Week 1	Week 2	Week 3	Week 4	Week 5
Opening inventory	2,000				
Production					
Sub-total					
Sales	14,000	16,000	15,000	14,000	16,000
Closing inventory					

Closing inventory should be 25% of the following week's forecast sales.

28 PRODUCT C

Complete the following production forecast for product C.

Units of product C	Week 1	Week 2	Week 3	Week 4	Week 5
Opening inventory	500				
Production					
Sub-total					
Sales	3,500	4,000	3,750	3,500	4,000
Closing inventory					

Closing inventory should be 20% of the following week's forecast sales.

(All gaps are numeric.)

29 PRODUCT B

The quarterly production requirements for product B are shown below.

5% of production fails the quality checks and must be scrapped.

How many items of product B must be manufactured to allow for waste?

	Month 1	Month 2	Month 3
Required units	90,250	95,000	99,750
Manufactured units			

30 ROPE

The quarterly production requirements for product 'Rope' are shown below.

5% of production fails the quality checks and must be scrapped.

How many items of 'Rope' must be manufactured to allow for waste?

	Month 1	Month 2	Month 3
Required units	180,670	190,980	185,900
Manufactured units			

31 CAMELIA

Labour hours

104,000 units of product 'Camelia' are to be manufactured in May. Each one takes 3 minutes to produce.

25 staff will each work 176 hours basic time.

How many overtime hours must be worked to complete the production?

Select from	600	5,200	860	800	3,800

32 SAGE

Raw material purchases

20,000 items of product Sage are to be manufactured in April. Each requires 2.5 metres of raw material. You are also told that:

- 20% of raw material is wasted during manufacture.

- The opening inventory will be 10,000 metres.

- The closing inventory will be 14,000 metres.

How much material must be purchased?

Select from	63,000m	66,500m	70,750m	52,000m	68,000m

33 BUMBLEBEE

The quarterly production requirements for product Bumblebee are shown below.

2% of production fails the quality checks and must be scrapped.

How many items of product B must be manufactured to allow for waste?

	Month 1	Month 2	Month 3
Required units	18,900	20,150	22,200
Manufactured units			

34 QUALITY CONTROL

The company has budgeted to make and sell 240,000 units in the coming year.

Each unit takes 1.5 labour hours to make and requires 2.5kg of raw material. The quality control department can test 18,000 units each month. A contract has been placed to purchase 500,000kg of raw material at an agreed price. Further supplies can be obtained on the open market but the price is likely to be much higher. The company employs 198 production workers. Each worker works 1,750 hours in a year in normal time.

Complete the following analysis.

There is labour available to make _____ units in normal time. Therefore, _____ hours of overtime will be needed.

The raw material contract will provide enough material to make _____ units. Therefore, _____ kg will have to be purchased on the open market.

Quality control can test _____ units in the year. It will be necessary to make alternative arrangements for _____ units.

35   COMPANY A

Company A has budgeted to make and sell 140,000 units in the coming year.

Each unit takes 1.2 labour hours to make and requires 1.8kg of raw material. The quality control department can test 10,000 units each month. A contract has been placed to purchase 180,000kg of raw material at an agreed price. Further supplies can be obtained on the open market but the price is likely to be much higher. The company employs 90 production workers. Each worker works 1,750 hours in a year in normal time.

Complete the following analysis.

There is labour available to make _____ units in normal time. Therefore, _____ hours of overtime will be needed.

The raw material contract will provide enough material to make _____ units. Therefore, _____ kg will have to be purchased on the open market.

Quality control can test _____ units in the year. It will be necessary to make alternative arrangements for _____ units.

36   JONES

Jones has budgeted to make and sell 150,000 units in the coming year.

Each unit takes 0.8 labour hours to make and requires 3kg of raw material. The quality control department can test 12,000 units each month. A contract has been placed to purchase 300,000kg of raw material at an agreed price. Further supplies can be obtained on the open market but the price is likely to be much higher. The company employs 60 production workers. Each worker works 1,750 hours in a year in normal time.

Complete the following analysis.

There is labour available to make _____ units in normal time. Therefore, _____ hours of overtime will be needed.

The raw material contract will provide enough material to make _____ units. Therefore, _____ kg will have to be purchased on the open market.

Quality control can test _____ units in the year. It will be necessary to make alternative arrangements for _____ units.

37   DONALD

Labour hours

84,000 units of product Donald are to be manufactured in May. Each one takes 3 minutes to produce.

25 staff will each work 160 hours basic time.

How many overtime hours must be worked to complete the production?

| **Select from** | 200 | 4,200 | 360 | 300 | 3,800 |

38   THEO

Labour hours

48,000 units of product 'Theo' are to be manufactured in May.

Each one takes 6 minutes to produce.

28 staff will each work 170 hours basic time.

How many overtime hours must be worked to complete the production?

Select from   200   4,800   4,760   300   40

MACHINE UTILISATION

39   E, F AND G

Department Y manufactures three products, E, F and G.

Calculate the machine hours required to manufacture these in November.

Product	Units	Hours per unit	Hours required
E	100	1.0	
F	230	2.0	
G	370	3.5	
Total hours for Department Y			

There are four machines in the department.

Each machine can be used for 300 hours in November. Additional machines can be hired if required.

How many additional machines should be hired?

40   ZEE

Zee manufactures three products, C, D and E.

Calculate the machine hours required to manufacture these in January.

Product	Units	Hours per unit	Hours required
C	200	0.5	
D	460	2.0	
E	740	2.5	
Total hours for Zee			

There are five machines in the department.

Each machine can be used for 500 hours in January. Additional machines can be hired if required.

How many additional machines should be hired?

41   CLAUDIO

Calculate machine utilisation.

Do not show decimals. Round up to the next whole number of hours or percentage, if necessary. There are 100 machines in the department. Each can be used for 80 hours in the period.

Budgeted machine loading	Items	Hours per item	Hours required
Product			
A	2,000	1.00	
B	1,750	2.00	
C	610	3.00	
Total machine hours required			
% utilisation			

42   DOGBERRY

Calculate machine utilisation.

Do not show decimals. Round up to the next whole number of hours or percentage, if necessary. There are 50 machines in the department. Each can be used for 50 hours in the period.

Budgeted machine loading	Items	Hours per item	Hours required
Product			
A	120	3.75	
B	175	1.50	
C	190	1.50	
Total machine hours required			
% utilisation			

43   LEONATO

Calculate machine utilisation.

Do not show decimals. Round up to the next whole number of hours or percentage, if necessary. There are 60 machines in the department. Each can be used for 40 hours in the period.

Budgeted machine loading	Items	Hours per item	Hours required
Product			
A	250	3.00	
B	1,000	1.00	
C	390	1.50	
Total machine hours required			
% utilisation			

44   BORACHIO

Calculate machine utilisation.

Do not show decimals. Round up to the next whole number of hours or percentage, if necessary.

There are 40 machines in the department. Each can be used for 5 hours in the period.

Budgeted machine loading	Items	Hours per item	Hours required
Product			
A	25	4	
B	10	2	
C	40	1.50	
Total machine hours required			
% utilisation			

CAPACITY CONSTRAINTS

45   GLOUCESTER

Calculate the capacity constraints for product FF by completing the table below.

Round down to the maximum whole number of units, if necessary.

According to the standard cost card, each unit of this product requires:

- 1 kilograms of material
- 40 minutes of direct labour time
- 5 minutes of machine time

Budgets have been drafted by departmental heads which show:

- Maximum sales demand of 1,700 units
- 2,500 kilograms of material available
- 420 hours of direct labour time available without using overtime
- 120 hours of machine time available.

Production capacity	Units
Sufficient materials are budgeted to manufacture	
Without overtime, sufficient direct labour is budgeted to manufacture	
Sufficient machine time is budgeted to manufacture	
Without overtime, the maximum sales volume is	
With unlimited overtime, the maximum sales volume is	

46 BEDFORD

Calculate the capacity constraints for product FF by completing the table below.

Round down to the maximum whole number of units, if necessary.

According to the standard cost card, each unit of this product requires:

- 12 kilograms of material
- 120 minutes of direct labour time
- 25 minutes of machine time

Budgets have been drafted by departmental heads which show:

- Maximum sales demand of 350 units
- 1,200 kilograms of material available
- 600 hours of direct labour time available without using overtime
- 180 hours of machine time available.

Production capacity	Units
Sufficient materials are budgeted to manufacture	
Without overtime, sufficient direct labour is budgeted to manufacture	
Sufficient machine time is budgeted to manufacture	
Without overtime, the maximum sales volume is	
With unlimited overtime, the maximum sales volume is	

WORKING SCHEDULES AND OPERATING BUDGETS

47   WASHINGTON

Complete the three working schedules using the information from the production budget and notes below.

Enter all figures as positive values.

Production budget	Units
Opening inventory of finished goods	1,050
Production	20,000
	————
Sub-total	21,050
Sales	18,000
	————
Closing inventory of finished goods	3,050
	————

Materials	Kg	£
Opening inventory	2,200	3,080
Purchases @ £1.50 per kg		
Sub-total		
Used		
Closing inventory	35,000	
Closing inventory to be valued at budgeted purchase price		

Materials
Each unit produced requires 2.5 kilograms of material.
Closing inventory is to be valued at the budgeted price per kilo.

Labour	Hours	£
Basic time @ £16 per hour		
Overtime		
Total		

Labour
Each item takes 6 minutes to produce.
8 staff work 200 basic hours each in the period.
Overtime is paid at time and a half (50% above basic rate).

Production overhead	Hours	£
Variable @ £2.50 per hour		
Fixed		165,020
Total		

Production overhead
Variable overhead is recovered on total labour hours.

48   ADAMS

Use the information provided in the previous question, 'Washington' to complete the operating budget below.

Enter income, costs and inventories as positive figures.

Closing finished goods inventory will be valued at the budgeted production cost per unit.

Operating budget	Units	£ per unit	£
Sales revenue		27.00	
Cost of goods sold			£
Opening inventory of finished goods			40,000
Cost of production		£	
Materials			
Labour			
Production overhead			
Closing inventory of finished goods			
Cost of goods sold			
Gross profit / (loss)			
Overheads		£	
Administration		80,000	
Marketing		25,000	
Operating profit / (loss)			

49   JEFFERSON

Complete the three working schedules using the information from the production budget and notes below.

Enter all figures as positive values.

Production budget	Units
Opening inventory of finished goods	3,000
Production	16,500
	———
Sub-total	19,500
Sales	15,000
	———
Closing inventory of finished goods	4,500
	———

Materials	Kg	£
Opening inventory	20,000	12,000
Purchases @ £2.00 per kg		
Sub-total		
Used		
Closing inventory	35,000	

Closing inventory to be valued at budgeted purchase price

Materials
Each unit produced requires 5 kilograms of material.
Closing inventory is to be valued at the budgeted price per kilo.

Labour	Hours	£
Basic time @ £8 per hour		
Overtime		
Total		

Labour
Each item takes 12 minutes to produce.
35 staff work 60 basic hours each in the period.
Overtime is paid at time and a half (50% above basic rate).

Production overhead	Hours	£
Variable @ £2.00 per hour		
Fixed		155,200
Total		

Production overhead
Variable overhead is recovered on total labour hours.

50   BURR

Use the information provided in the previous question, 'Jefferson' to complete the operating budget below.

Enter income, costs and inventories as positive figures.

Closing finished goods inventory will be valued at the budgeted production cost per unit.

Operating budget	Units	£ per unit	£
Sales revenue		30.00	
Cost of goods sold			£
Opening inventory of finished goods			40,000
Cost of production		£	
Materials			
Labour			
Production overhead			
Closing inventory of finished goods			
Cost of goods sold			
Gross profit / (loss)			
Overheads		£	
Administration		55,000	
Marketing		60,000	
Operating profit / (loss)			

51   JUNEAU

You work for Juneau Ltd as a management accountant. The company makes two products, the Key and the Jet, that are sold to the water management industry. Both products use the same type of materials and labour, but in different quantities.

The company operates a five-day week for both production and sales and divides its year into five-week periods.

One of your jobs is to prepare the production budget. You are given the following information to help you to prepare this budget for the five weeks ending 22nd December 2010.

Forecast sales volumes (units)	Key	Jet
Period 11: 5 weeks to 22 December 2010	9,350	10,120
Period 12: 5 weeks to 1 February 2010	11,275	12,925

Inventories

Finished goods inventory at the beginning of period 11 will be 1103 Keys, and 1305 Jets; there are no inventories of raw materials or work in progress.

The unit full absorption cost of finished goods inventories at the beginning of period 11 will be £51 for a Key, and £66 for a Jet. The finished goods inventory of Keys at the end of period 11 must be equal to 3 working days sales of Keys in period 12; the finished goods inventory of Jets at the end of period 11 must be equal to 5 working days sales of Jets in period 12.

Materials

Each Key requires 11 kg of material and each Jet 14 kg of material. The cost of the material is £6 per kg, and 3% of material is lost through wastage during production. This loss has no scrap value.

Labour

Juneau employs 23 production employees who work a standard 35-hour week. 8 Keys can be made in one labour hour and 4 Jets can be made in one labour hour. The basic labour rate is £8 per hour and overtime is paid at a premium of 50% of this rate per hour. Any overtime premium is charged to production overheads rather than to the cost of direct labour.

Production overheads

Overheads are charged to production at the rate of £15 per labour hour.

Required:

1   **Prepare the following information for period 11 (the five weeks to 22nd December 2010):**

    (a)   **production budget in units for the Key and the Jet**

    (b)   **material purchases budget in kilograms**

    (c)   **cost of material purchases budget**

    (d)   **direct labour hours budget**

    (e)   **cost of direct labour budget**

    (f)   **total cost of production based on full absorption costing**

    (g)   **cost of opening finished goods inventories, based on full absorption costing.**

2   The Sales Director at Juneau, Alex Dell, has just informed you that he has negotiated a new order and wants you to increase your budget to produce an extra 2,000 Keys and 2,000 Jets in period 11.

You are told that due to sickness, the total number of production employees available for period 11 will be reduced by three. The maximum number of overtime hours available in any five-week period is 60 hours per employee.

You are also aware that due to a transport problem, the maximum amount of additional material available to meet the increase in production is 52,000 kg. There can be no change in finished inventory, and the wastage rate cannot be improved.

Write a memo to Axel Dell regarding the feasibility of producing the extra Keys and Jets for the order. You should include the following:

(a) calculations to show whether there is any restriction on the extra production of Keys and Jets due to:

(i) labour

(ii) materials.

(b) a revised production budget in units for both Keys and Jets in order to meet the new order.

(c) TWO recommendations in order to meet the production requirements of this new order.

52 SINCLAIR LTD

Sinclair Ltd makes a single product, the Dom. You are Sinclair's management accountant and you are responsible for preparing its operating budgets. The accounting year is divided into 13 four-week periods. There are five days in each week. The sales director of Sinclair has recently completed the following forecast sales volume for the next five periods:

Sales forecast five periods to 18 November 2011

	Period 1	Period 2	Period 3	Period 4	Period 5
4 weeks ending	29 July	26 August	23 Sept	21 Oct	18 Nov
Number of Doms	19,400	21,340	23,280	22,310	22,310

The production director also provides you with the following information:

(i) On completion of production, 3% of the Doms are found to be faulty and have to be scrapped. The faulty Doms are thought to be caused by poor work practices by some of the production workers although this is not known for certain.

The faulty Doms have no scrap value.

(ii) Opening inventories in period 1 were made of finished goods (3,880 Doms) and raw materials (16,500 litres).

(iii) Closing inventories at the end of each period have set rules: finished inventory must equal four days' sales volume of Doms in the next period, and raw materials must equal five days' gross production in the next period.

(iv) Each Dom requires 3 litres of material costing £8 per litre.

(v) Each Dom requires 0.5 hours of labour.

(vi) Sinclair employs 70 production workers who each work a 40-hour week. The 70 production workers work independently of one another in making Doms. Each employee is paid a guaranteed wage of £240 per week, and overtime payments should only be made if absolutely necessary.

(vii) The cost of any overtime is £9 per hour.

Required:

1   Prepare the following budgets for the production director:

(a)   *Gross production budget* in Doms (including faulty production) for each of the first four periods.

(b)   *Material purchases budget* in litres for each of the first three periods.

(c)   *Cost of the material purchases* for each of the first three periods.

(d)   *Labour budget* in hours for each of the first three periods including any overtime required in each period.

(e)   *Cost of the labour budget* for each of the first three periods including the cost of any overtime.

2   Write a short memo to the production director. In your memo, you should:

(a)   explain and quantify the value of any possible overtime savings.

(b)   suggest ONE extra cost which might be necessary to achieve the overtime savings.

CASH FLOW FORECASTS

53   **WASHINGTON AND ADAMS**

Complete the cash flow forecast using the budget data that you have calculated in questions 47 'Washington' and 48 'Adams', as well as the information below. Enter receipts and payments as positive figures.

The sales receivables balance is expected to decrease by 162,000 over the year.

The materials payable balance is expected to increase by 26,800 over the year.

All other payments are made in the year in which they are incurred.

Production overheads include a depreciation charge of 19,000.

Cash flow forecast	£	
Opening cash balance / (overdraft)		29,650
Sales receipts		
Payments		
Materials		
Labour		
Production overhead		
Other overheads		
Capital expenditure	50,000	
Closing cash balance / (overdraft)		

54   JEFFERSON AND BURR

Complete the cash flow forecast using the budget data that you have calculated in questions 49 'Jefferson' and 50 'Burr', as well as the information below. Enter receipts and payments as positive figures.

The sales receivables balance is expected to decrease by 15,000 over the year.

The materials payable balance is expected to decrease by 32,600 over the year.

All other payments are made in the year in which they are incurred.

Production overheads include a depreciation charge of 15,000.

Cash flow forecast	£	
Opening cash balance / (overdraft)		90,000
Sales receipts		
Payments		
Materials		
Labour		
Production overhead		
Other overheads		
Capital expenditure	120,000	
Closing cash balance / (overdraft)		

55   CASH FORECAST FOR MAY

Prepare a cash forecast for May from the following budget data.

Budget data	Feb £	Mar £	Apr £	May £	Cash forecast	May £
Invoiced sales	7,000	7,700	7,900	8,300	Opening cash balance	−320
Purchases	6,500	6,300	6,400	6,700	Customer receipts	
Wages	300	340	370	400		
Other overheads	550	540	575	590	**Payments**	
Capital expenditure	0	0	0	3,000	For purchases	
					For wages	
Average terms					For overheads	
55% of customers take 1 month to pay, the remainder take 2 months					For capital exp.	
Purchases paid for in the current month					Total	
Wages paid in the current month						
Other overheads paid after two months					Closing cash balance	
Capital expenditure paid in the following month						

Show payments and receipts as plus figures.

Negative balance = overdrawn

56   THE LATEST

Prepare the forecast from the operating budget and balance sheet assumptions.

Enter receipts and payments as positive figures.

Balance sheet assumptions:

Receivables will increase by £90,000.

Materials payables will reduce by £77,000.

Labour costs are paid in the period in which they are incurred.

Other payables will increase by £2,000.

Operating budget	£	£
Sales revenue		352,000
Expenditure		
Materials	34,200	
Labour	41,250	
Other costs	16,400	91,850
Operating profit		260,150

Cash flow forecast	£	£
Sales receipts		
Payments		
Materials		
Labour		
Other costs		
Cash-flow forecast		

57   HARVEST FESTIVAL

Prepare the forecast from the operating budget and balance sheet assumptions.

Enter receipts and payments as positive figures.

Balance sheet assumptions:

Receivables will reduce by £1,500.

Materials payables will increase by £2,500.

Labour costs are paid in the period in which they are incurred.

Other payables will reduce by £650.

Operating budget	£	£
Sales revenue		112,000
Expenditure		
Materials	35,000	
Labour	26,200	
Other costs	16,700	77,900
Operating profit		34,100

Cash flow forecast	£	£
Sales receipts		
Payments		
Materials		
Labour		
Other costs		
Cash-flow forecast		

58 OKTOBERFEST

Prepare the forecast from the operating budget and balance sheet assumptions.

Enter receipts and payments as positive figures.

Balance sheet assumptions:

Receivables will increase by £3,000.

Materials payables will increase by £3,000.

Labour costs are paid in the period in which they are incurred.

Other payables will reduce by £3,150.

Operating budget	£	£
Sales revenue		159,800
Expenditure		
Materials	58,550	
Labour	20,000	
Other costs	19,300	97,850
Operating profit		61,950

Cash flow forecast	£	£
Sales receipts		
Payments		
Materials		
Labour		
Other costs		
Cash Flow forecast		

PERIODIC BUDGETS

59 APRIL BUDGETS

Calculate these sales and cost budgets for April:

	Budget for the year	Budget for April
Units sold	34,000	3,000
Units produced	36,000	3,500
	£	£
Sales	204,000	
Materials used	59,400	
Labour	67,200	
Variable production overhead	54,000	
Fixed overhead	3,600	

Each unit is made from 1.5 kg of material costing £1.10 per kg.

It takes 6 minutes to make each item. 200 hours of basic time is available in the month. Any extra hours must be worked in overtime.

The basic rate is £16 per hour. Overtime is paid at time and a half (50% more than basic rate.) Variable overhead relates to labour hours, including overtime. Fixed overhead costs are incurred evenly through the year.

60 ROSE

Rose Ltd manufactures a single product, the Bud.

Calculate these sales and cost budgets for May:

	Budget for the year	Budget for May
Units sold	68,000	6,000
Units produced	72,000	7,000
	£	£
Sales	1,408,000	
Materials used	720,000	
Labour	264,000	
Variable production overhead	96,000	
Fixed overhead	3,600	

Each Bud is made from 2.5 kg of material costing £4 per kg. It takes 10 minutes to make a Bud.

800 hours of basic time is available in the month. Any extra hours must be worked in overtime.

The basic rate is £20 per hour. Overtime is paid at time and a half (50% more than basic rate.)

Variable overhead relates to labour hours, including overtime.

Fixed overhead costs are incurred evenly through the year.

Round to nearest whole number.

61 SALES AND COSTS

Calculate these sales and cost budgets for June:

	Budget for the year	Budget for June
Units sold	120,000	11,000
Units produced	110,000	10,000
	£	£
Sales	1,649,000	
Materials used	1,155,000	
Labour	95,500	
Variable production overhead	55,000	
Fixed overhead	3,600	

Each unit is made from 3.5 kg of material costing £3 per kg.

It takes 5 minutes to make each item.

700 hours of basic time is available in the month.

Any extra hours must be worked in overtime.

The basic rate is £10 per hour.

Overtime is paid at time and a half (50% more than basic rate.)

Variable overhead relates to labour hours, including overtime.

Fixed overhead costs are incurred evenly through the year.

ALTERNATIVE SCENARIOS

62   MADISON

Complete the alternative scenario column in the operating budget table and calculate the increase or decrease in profit.

For the sales price per unit figure, enter any decimal places, if relevant.

For the other figures, round to the nearest whole number, if necessary.

Assumptions in the first scenario

Material and labour costs are variable.

Depreciation is a stepped cost, increasing at every 8,000 units.

There is an allowance for an energy rise of 10.0%.

Alternative scenario

Increase the selling price by 5.0%

Reduce the sales volume by 8.0%.

Revise the energy price rise to 8.0%.

Operating budget	First draft	Alternative scenario
Sales price per unit (£)	15.00	
Sales volume	75,000	
		£
Sales revenue	1,125,000	
Costs		
Material	131,250	
Labour	187,500	
Energy	44,000	
Depreciation	62,400	
Total	425,150	
Gross Profit	699,850	
Increase / (decrease) in gross profit		

63   MONROE

Complete the alternative scenario column in the operating budget table and calculate the increase or decrease in profit.

For the sales price per unit figure, enter any decimal places, if relevant.

For the other figures, round to the nearest whole number, if necessary.

Assumptions in the first scenario

Material and labour costs are variable.

Depreciation is a stepped cost, increasing at every 1,000 units.

There is an allowance for an energy rise of 10.0%.

Alternative scenario

Increase the selling price by 5.0%.

Reduce the sales volume by 2.0%.

Revise the energy price rise to 3.0%.

Operating budget	First draft	Alternative scenario
Sales price per unit (£)	20.00	
Sales volume	6,200	
		£
Sales revenue	124,000	
Costs		
Material	4,650	
Labour	12,400	
Energy	33,000	
Depreciation	14,000	
Total	64,050	
Gross Profit	59,950	
Increase / (decrease) in gross profit		

SALES REVENUE AND COSTS FORECASTS

64 INCOME FORECAST (I)

From the following data revise the income forecast.

Next year, income is forecast at £4,284,000. This assumes a 2% increase in selling price. In the light of increasing competition the marketing manager has decided not to make the increase.

The forecast should be revised to _____.

Select from   £4,198,320   £4,200,000   £4,284,000   £4,369,680

65 INCOME FORECAST (II)

From the following data revise the income forecast.

Next year income is forecast at £7,272,000. This assumes a 1% increase in selling price.

In the light of increasing competition the marketing manager has decided not to make the increase.

The forecast should be revised to _____.

Select from   £7,199,280   £7,200,000   £7,272,000   £7,344,720

66   **INCOME FORECAST (III)**

From the following data revise the income forecast.

Next year income is forecast at £816,000. This assumes a 2% increase in selling price.

In the light of increasing competition the marketing manager has decided not to make the increase.

The forecast should be revised to _____.

Select from   £799,680   £800,000   £816,000   £832,320

67   **ENERGY COSTS**

From the following data revise the forecast for energy costs.

Next year energy costs are forecast at £157,590. This assumes a 3% increase in energy consumption and a 2% increase in gas and electricity tariffs.

However energy saving measures are being proposed. Instead of increasing, consumption should be reduced by 6%.

The energy budget should be £_____.

Select from   £143,820   £148,135   £150,000   £153,000

68   **ELECTRICITY COSTS**

From the following data revise the forecast for electricity costs.

Next year energy costs are forecast at £212,160. This assumes a 2% increase in energy consumption and a 4% increase in gas and electricity tariffs.

However energy saving measures are being proposed. Instead of increasing, consumption should be reduced by 5%.

The energy budget should be £_____.

Select from   £197,600   £200,000   £201,552   £208,000

69   **FORECASTS**

This year sales are £2,000,000.

Analysis of recent years shows a growth trend of 10% per annum.

The seasonal variation has been:

- quarter 1   +£35,000
- quarter 2   +£20,000
- quarter 3   −£10,000
- quarter 4   −£45,000

Forecast the income for each quarter of next year.

Quarter	£
1	
2	
3	
4	
Year	

70 FLUTE

This year sales are £4,000,000.

Analysis of recent years shows a growth trend of 20% per annum.

The seasonal variation has been:

* quarter 1   +£30,000

* quarter 2   +£50,000

* quarter 3   +£135,000

* quarter 4   −£215,000

Forecast the income for each quarter of next year.

Quarter	£
1	
2	
3	
4	
Year	

SAMPLING

71 STRATIFIED SAMPLING

Calculate the number of customers to be interviewed from each age group to obtain a representative response from 1,000 interviews.

Do not show decimals. Round to the nearest whole number.

Age range	Up to 29	30 to 39	40 to 49	Over 49	Total
Number of customers	23,500	24,000	41,500	54,000	
Sample					

72 HOURS IN A DAY

Calculate the number of customers to be interviewed from each age group to obtain a representative response from 2,000 interviews.

Do not show decimals. Round to the nearest whole number.

Age range	Up to 29	30 to 39	40 to 49	Over 49	Total
Number of customers	69,500	57,000	42,500	12,200	
Sample					

73 PARIS KITCHEN

Calculate the number of customers to be interviewed from each age group to obtain a representative response from 100 interviews.

Do not show decimals. Round to the nearest whole number.

Age range	Up to 29	30 to 39	40 to 49	Over 49	Total
Number of customers	25,500	32,000	42,000	54,000	
Sample					

74   **RACHEL**

Calculate the number of customers to be interviewed from each age group to obtain a representative response from 250 interviews.

Do not show decimals. Round to the nearest whole number.

Age range	Up to 29	30 to 39	40 to 49	Over 49	Total
Number of customers	1,300	5,900	5,700	5,000	
Sample					

75   **SAMPLING ARMISTICE**

Calculate the number of customers to be interviewed from each age group to obtain a representative response from 1,500 interviews.

Do not show decimals. Round to the nearest whole number.

Age range	Up to 29	30 to 39	40 to 49	Over 49	Total
Number of customers	16,000	22,000	45,000	20,000	
Sample					

76   **ADVENT**

Calculate the number of customers to be interviewed from each age group to obtain a representative response from 2,500 interviews.

Do not show decimals. Round to the nearest whole number.

Age range	Up to 29	30 to 39	40 to 49	Over 49	Total
Number of customers	15,000	15,500	15,000	15,600	
Sample					

WRITTEN EMAIL TASKS

77   NOSEY

You are asked to review the Operating Statement for Nosey Ltd, shown below, and the background information provided, and to make recommendations.

Operating Statement for May 2009

	Revenue (units)		3,264,000

	Budget	Actual	Variance Fav/(Adverse)
	£	£	£
Revenue	6,528,000	7,180,800	652,800
Variable costs			
Material	1,958,400	1,960,200	(1,800)
Labour	1,468,800	1,542,200	(73,400)
Distribution	260,400	266,600	(6,200)
Power	326,400	324,700	1,700
Equipment hire	163,200	162,000	1,200
	4,177,200	4,255,700	(78,500)
Contribution	2,350,800	2,925,100	574,300
Fixed costs			
Power	33,600	36,000	(2,400)
Equipment hire	24,000	21,600	2,400
Depreciation	259,200	264,000	(4,800)
Marketing	290,400	307,200	(16,800)
Administration	352,800	362,400	(9,600)
	960,000	991,200	(31,200)
Operating profit	1,390,800	1,933,900	543,100

The budget has been flexed to the actual number of units produced and sold. The original budget had been drawn up by the Chief Executive of Nosey and communicated to senior managers by email.

Despite an unbudgeted price increase, the volume of units sold was higher than expected in the original budget. This seems to have been due to a very successful advertising campaign. Unfortunately, the extra demand could only be met by the work force working overtime, which is paid at time and a half.

One of the raw materials included in the product is a chemical which fell in price by 3% for part of the month.

Although pleased with the overall results, the Chief Executive is concerned that costs were above budget and has asked you to advise how control can be improved.

Write an email to the Chief Executive in which you:

(a)   Suggest possible reasons for the variances on materials, labour, marketing and administration

(b)   Explain THREE steps that the company can take to motivate managers to achieve budgets.

To	Chief executive	**Date**	(Today)
From	Budget accountant	**Subject**	Review of operating statement

(a)   Reasons for variances

(b)   Three steps to motivate managers to achieve budgets

78   CM LTD

The directors of CM Ltd are putting forward a budget proposal for 2017. Actual results for 2016 are provided for comparison. The Chief Exec's approval of the 2017 budget is requested. You are CM's budget accountant.

Substantial sales growth was achieved in 2016. CM Ltd introduced more than a dozen innovative new products. The key features of these products are patented and therefore protected from direct competition. CM Ltd has a solid customer base.

In 2017, CM Ltd will retain its own identity in the market place. In addition, CM's directors plan to develop a sales channel through George Products Ltd and to be promoted in that company's catalogue.

CM Ltd has 50 products in its catalogue at all stages of the product lifecycle. More exciting new products are being planned. CM's directors are confident that the budgeted 10% growth will be achieved. They have explained that they do not feel it is realistic to try and calculate sales revenue and costs at product level.

The directors have also allowed a 2.5% increase in costs in line with expected inflation. A yearly management bonus (£21,000 in 2016) is linked to these 2017 results, but it has not yet been authorised for payment by the company's remuneration committee.

No increase in selling prices has been assumed, because this is difficult to achieve with high-tech products.

Operating budget for year ended 31/12/2017	2016 results	Draft 2017 budget
Sales volume	7,950	8,745
	£	£
Sales revenue	1,128,900	1,241,790
Costs:		
Materials	246,450	277,256
Labour	409,425	460,603
Production overheads	144,690	162,776
Depreciation	46,800	52,650
Marketing	18,640	20,970
Administration	92,600	104,175
Total	958,605	1,078,430
Operating profit	170,295	163,360
Operating profit as a % to sales	15.1%	13.2%

Write an email to the Chief Executive in which you:

(a)   Examine the planning assumptions and calculations in the proposed budget, and identify any weaknesses.

(b)   Explain how costs and profitability should be managed in a multi-product manufacturing organisation

(c)   Give your opinion, with reasons, on how well the budget would motivate managers to create sustainable, profitable growth.

79   CONTROLLABILITY

Rough & Tumble (R&T) manufactures children's sports clothes for sale online. In the factory, nylon is mostly used in the manufacturing process.

Jon McRae has just joined R&T as Production Manager and has argued that R&T should only use cotton in production, as cotton is superior to nylon for exercise as it 'breathes' more easily. However, cotton is more expensive than nylon. Jon McRae hopes the increased quality of the clothes would stimulate demand, and justify an immediate price increase for the clothes.

R&T operates a responsibility accounting system, which updates raw materials standards every December and allocates variances to specific individuals. Bonuses are only awarded to managers when favourable variances are allocated to them.

Jon Mc Rae's approach was approved and only pure cotton clothes were manufactured from the start of March 2010, although no changes were made to the standard cost cards.

You are the Assistant Management Accountant in R&T and you have been presented with the following extract from a variance report:

Manager responsible:	Allocated variances	February	March
Production manager	Material price (total for all materials)	£ 300 F	£ (3,000) A
	Material usage	£ 100 F	£ (200) A
Sales manager	Sales variance	£ (700) A	£ 10,000 F

Required:

Write an email to the Chief Executive in which you:

(a)   **Assess the performance of the Production Manager and that of the Sales Manager.**

(b)   **Comment on the controllability of variances in R&T and the fairness of the bonus scheme.**

To	Chief executive	**Date**	(Today)
From	Assistant Management Accountant	**Subject**	Review of variances

(a) **Performance of production manager and sales manager**

(b) **Controllability of variances in R&T and the fairness of the bonus scheme**

80   FRANKA

You are asked to review the operating statement shown below, and the background information provided, and to make recommendations.

Operating statement for May 2009

Revenue (units)			380,000
	Budget	**Actual**	**Variance Fav/(Adverse)**
	£	£	£
Revenue	8,740,000	8,626,000	(114,000)
Variable costs			
Material	2,040,000	2,116,000	(76,000)
Labour	1,900,000	1,938,000	(38,000)
Distribution	126,000	127,000	(1,000)
Power	1,720,000	1,624,000	96,000
Equipment hire	87,400	86,100	1,300
	5,873,400	5,891,100	(17,700)
Contribution	2,866,600	2,734,900	(131,700)
Fixed costs			
Power	160,000	150,700	9,300
Equipment hire	20,000	21,500	(1,500)
Depreciation	400,000	200,000	200,000
Marketing	480,000	358,000	122,000
Administration	438,600	432,200	6,400
	1,498,600	1,162,400	336,200
Operating profit	1,368,000	1,572,500	204,500

The budget has been flexed to the actual number of units produced and sold. The original budget had been drawn up by the Chief Executive and communicated to senior managers by email. This was part of a new performance-related pay scheme recently introduced for senior managers.

For technical reasons, the same amount of electricity is required for each unit produced and no economies are possible. There is only one possible electricity supplier who has recently reduced both its fixed charge and its variable charge per unit.

The Chief Executive is pleased with the overall results and believes that it was the introduction of the performance-related pay that was the key reason for the actual profit being greater than forecast.

Write an email to the Chief Executive in which you:

(a) Explain the key variances and give reasons, other than performance-related pay, to explain why the actual profit for the year was greater than planned.

(b) Give FOUR general conditions necessary for performance-related pay to successfully lead to improved performance in organisations.

To	Chief executive	Date	(Today)
From	Budget accountant	Subject	Review of operating statement

(a) Key variances and reasons for increase in the actual profit

(b) FOUR general conditions necessary for performance-related pay to successfully lead to improved performance in organisations

81   LABOUR COSTS

You have prepared a draft budget for direct labour costs.

- It is based on this year's costs plus an expected pay rise and increased staffing.
- The manager of human resources has forecast the pay rise.
- You have calculated the required staffing from the agreed production budget.
- You have been asked to suggest appropriate performance measures that would assist managers to monitor direct labour performance against budget.

Direct labour budget

	This year	Next year budget
Production units	1,170,000	1,650,000
Minutes per unit	5.00	5.00
Labour hours	97,500	137,500
Annual hrs per staff member	1,700	1,700
Number of staff	58	81
Average salary p.a.	£30,000	£31,500
Direct labour cost	£1,740,000	£2,551,500

Write an email to the Production director:

(a)   Explaining the calculations and assumptions and requesting his approval

(b)   Suggesting appropriate direct labour performance indicators for this department

To	Production director	**Date**	(Today)
From	Budget accountant	**Subject**	Direct labour budget

(a)   Budget submission

(b)   Performance indicators

82   X AND Z

X Ltd and Z Ltd are potential new customers for your business. The financial information below has been supplied by X and Z Limited and you are trying to establish the creditworthiness of both businesses:

Accounts for X Limited	2009	2008
	£000	£000
Revenue	**4,500**	**5,500**
Cost of sales	3,500	3,800
Gross profit	**1,000**	**1,700**
Distribution costs	1,050	1,150
Administration costs	1,000	1,000
Operating profit	**−1,050**	**−450**
Finance costs	100	50
Profit on ordinary activities before taxation	**−1,150**	**−500**
Tax on profit on ordinary activities	0	0
Profit for the financial year	**−1,150**	**−500**
Balance sheet	**2009**	**2008**
	£000	£000
Non-current assets		
Tangible assets	**2,200**	**2,500**
Current assets		
Inventories	900	750
Trade receivables	1,000	850
Cash	50	400
	1,950	**2,000**
Current liabilities		
Trade payables	2,100	1,800
Net current assets	**−150**	**200**
Non-current liabilities		
Long term loans	1,000	500
Net assets	**1,050**	**2,200**
Capital and reserves		
Share capital	200	200
Income statement	850	2,000
Shareholders' funds	**1,050**	**2,200**

Accounts for Z limited	2009	2008
	£000	£000
Revenue	**9,000**	**8,000**
Cost of sales	6,250	6,000
Gross profit	**2,750**	**2,000**
Distribution costs	850	850
Administration costs	600	600
Operating profit	**1,300**	**550**
Finance costs	250	250
Profit on ordinary activities before taxation	**1,050**	**300**
Tax on profit on ordinary activities	350	100
Profit for the financial year	**700**	**200**
Balance sheet	**2009**	**2008**
	£000	£000
Fixed assets		
Tangible assets	**4,500**	**3,900**
Current assets		
Inventories	1,200	1,000
Trade receivables	700	600
Cash	400	400
	2,300	**2,000**
Current liabilities		
Trade payables	1,500	1,300
Net current assets	**800**	**700**
Non-current liabilities		
Long term loans	2,500	2,500
Net assets	**2,800**	**2,100**
Capital and reserves		
Share capital	100	100
Income Statement	2,700	2000
Shareholders' funds	**2,800**	**2,100**

Required:

Using the templates provided, calculate the key indicators for 2008 and 2009 for X Limited and Z Limited.

(Answer to two decimal places.)

X Limited	Indicator	Indicator
Year	**2009**	**2008**
Operating profit margin		
Interest cover		
Current ratio		

Z Limited	Indicator	Indicator
Year	**2009**	**2008**
Operating profit margin		
Interest cover		
Current ratio		

83 DIEGO

You have prepared a draft budget for direct labour costs.

- Tough economic conditions are likely to hit the firms' sales and profit forecasts.

- It is based on this year's costs minus an expected pay cut and reduced staffing.

- The manager of human resources has forecast the pay cut.

- An increase in productivity is required to help cope with the adverse conditions.

- You have calculated the required staffing from the agreed production budget.

- You have been asked to suggest appropriate performance measures that would assist managers to monitor direct labour performance against budget.

Direct labour budget	Current year	Next year
Prod'n units	1,200,000	950,000
Minutes per unit	6	5.4
Labour hours	120,000	85,500
Annual hrs per staff member	1,800	1,860
Number of staff	67	46
Average salary pa	£35,000	£34,000
Direct labour cost	£2,345,000	£1,564,000

(a) Write an email to the production director explaining the calculations and assumptions and requesting his approval.

(b) Suggest some overall financial performance indicators for the firm.

To	Production director	**Date**	(Today)
From	Budget accountant	**Subject**	Direct labour budget

(a)   Budget submission

(b)   Performance indicators (no reference to above numbers required)

84   DRAFT BUDGET

You have prepared a draft budget for direct labour costs.

*   It is based on this year's costs plus an expected pay rise and increased staffing.

*   There is a favourable economic climate and the sales are forecast to rise.

*   The manager of human resources has forecast the pay rise due to labour market shortages.

*   Senior management have requested productivity to increase.

*   You have calculated the required staffing from the agreed production budget.

*   You have been asked to suggest appropriate performance measures that would assist managers to monitor direct labour performance against budget.

Direct labour budget	Current year	Next year
Prod'n units	1,200,000	1,500,000
Minutes per unit	10	9.5
Labour hours	200,000	237,500
Annual hrs per staff member	4,650	4,650
Number of staff	44	52
Average salary pa	£34,000	£36,000
Direct labour cost	£1,496,000	£1,872,000

Write an email to the production director:

(a)   Explaining the calculations and assumptions and requesting his approval

(b)   Suggesting appropriate direct labour performance indicators for this department

To	Production director	Date	(Today)
From	Budget accountant	**Subject**	Direct labour budget

(a)   Budget submission

(b)   Performance indicators

BUDGET REVISION, VARIANCE ANALYSIS

85 ST DAVIDS

Product X has a standard material cost as follows:

10 kilograms of material Y at £10 per kilogram = £100 per unit of X.

During February 2014, 1,000 units of X were manufactured, using 11,700 kilograms of material Y which cost £98,631.

Calculate the following variances:

(a) The material total variance

(b) The material price variance

(c) The material usage variance

86 EASTER FUN

Prepare the raw material cost statement from the activity data provided.

Activity data	Items produced	Kgs used	Cost
Budget	63,000	31,500	126,000
Actual results	65,000	33,500	112,000

Raw material cost statement	£
Standard raw material cost of production	
Variance (adverse shown as negative)	£ FAV/ – ADV
Material price	
Material usage	
Material cost	

87 ANNIVERSARY

Prepare the raw material cost statement from the activity data provided.

Activity data	Items produced	Kgs used	Cost
Budget	1,200	1,200	12,000
Actual results	1,250	1,300	15,000

Raw material cost statement	£
Standard raw material cost of production	
Variance (adverse shown as negative)	£ FAV/ – ADV
Material price	
Material usage	
Material cost	

88 APPLES AND PEARS

Prepare the raw material cost statement from the activity data provided.

Activity data	Items produced	Kgs used	Cost
Budget	78,000	109,200	65,520
Actual Results	81,500	120,000	83,250

Raw material cost statement	£
Standard raw material cost of production	
Variance (adverse shown as negative)	£ FAV/ – ADV
Material price	
Material usage	
Material cost	

89 INDEPENDENCE DAY

Prepare the raw material cost statement from the activity data provided.

Activity data	Items produced	Kgs used	Cost
Budget	126,000	100,800	50,400
Actual results	130,500	120,000	56,000

Raw material cost statement	£
Standard raw material cost of production	
Variance (adverse shown as negative)	£ FAV/ – ADV
Material price	
Material usage	
Material cost	

90 AUGUST

Prepare the raw material cost statement from the activity data provided.

Activity data	Items produced	Kgs used	Cost
Budget	1,500	4,500	9,000
Actual results	1,550	4,500	9,210

Raw material cost statement	£
Standard raw material cost of production	
Variance (adverse shown as negative)	£ FAV/ – ADV
Material price	
Material usage	
Material cost	

91   BIRTHDAY

Prepare the direct labour cost statement from the activity data provided.

Activity data	Items produced	Hours	Cost
Budget	10,000	7,500	150,000
Actual results	11,000	8,000	168,000

Enter favourable variances as positive figures, for example 500.

Enter adverse variances as negative figures, for example –500.

Direct labour cost statement	£
Standard direct labour cost of production	
Variance (adverse shown as negative)	
Labour rate	
Labour efficiency	
Labour cost	

92   VALENTINE

Prepare the direct labour cost statement from the activity data provided

Activity data	Items produced	Hours	Cost
Budget	6,450	64,500	612,750
Actual results	6,200	62,890	596,412

Enter favourable variances as positive figures, for example 500.

Enter adverse variances as negative figures, for example –500.

Direct labour cost statement	£
Standard direct labour cost of production	
Variance (adverse shown as negative)	
Labour rate	
Labour efficiency	
Labour cost	

MONTHLY OPERATING REPORTS, VARIANCE CALCULATIONS

93   OS

A monthly operating statement is shown below with some explanatory notes.

You are required to flex the budget, calculate variances and show whether each variance is favourable or adverse.

Monthly operating statement

	Budget	Actual
Volume	76,000	72,000
	£	£
Revenue	3,420,000	3,312,000
Costs		
Material	912,000	836,000
Labour	532,000	509,000
Distribution	19,000	19,500
Energy	215,000	201,250
Equipment hire	48,000	42,000
Depreciation	212,000	206,000
Marketing	268,000	255,000
Administration	184,000	190,000
Total	2,390,000	2,258,750
Operating profit	1,030,000	1,053,250

Monthly operating statement

	Flexed Budget £	Actual £	Variance Fav/(Adv) £
Volume	72,000		
Revenue		3,312,000	
Costs			
Material		836,000	
Labour		509,000	
Distribution		19,500	
Energy		201,250	
Equipment hire		42,000	
Depreciation		206,000	
Marketing		255,000	
Administration		190,000	
Total		2,258,750	
Operating profit		1,053,250	

Enter adverse variances as minus

Notes:

Material, labour and distribution costs are variable.

The budget for energy is semi-variable. The variable element is £2.50 per unit.

The budget for equipment hire is stepped, increasing at every 15,000 units of monthly production.

Depreciation, marketing and administration costs are fixed.

94 OS2

A monthly operating statement is shown below with some explanatory notes.

You are required to flex the budget, calculate variances and show whether each variance is favourable or adverse.

Monthly operating statement

	Budget	Actual
Volume	76,000	80,000
	£	£
Revenue	3,420,000	3,520,000
Costs		
Material	912,000	945,000
Labour	532,000	570,000
Distribution	19,000	19,500
Energy	215,000	219,250
Equipment hire	48,000	50,000
Depreciation	212,000	215,000
Marketing	268,000	253,000
Administration	184,000	166,000
Total	2,390,000	2,437,750
Operating profit	1,030,000	1,082,250

Monthly operating statement

Volume 80,000

	Flexed Budget	Actual	Variance Fav/(Adv)
	£	£	£
Revenue		3,520,000	
Costs			
Material		945,000	
Labour		570,000	
Distribution		19,500	
Energy		219,250	
Equipment hire		50,000	
Depreciation		215,000	
Marketing		253,000	
Administration		166,000	
Total		2,437,750	
Operating profit		1,082,250	

Enter adverse variances as minus

Notes:

Material, labour and distribution costs are variable.

The budget for energy is semi-variable. The variable element is £2.50 per unit.

The budget for equipment hire is stepped, increasing at every 15,000 units of monthly production.

Depreciation, marketing and administration costs are fixed.

95 OS3

A monthly operating statement is shown below with some explanatory notes.

You are required to flex the budget, calculate variances and show whether each variance is favourable or adverse.

Monthly operating statement

	Budget	Actual
Volume	120,000	110,000
	£	£
Revenue	2,400,000	2,255,000
Costs		
Material	480,000	425,000
Labour	180,000	149,000
Distribution	12,000	12,500
Energy	114,000	110,250
Equipment hire	25,000	32,000
Depreciation	145,000	148,000
Marketing	260,000	255,000
Administration	172,000	181,000
Total	1,388,000	1,312,750
Operating profit	1,012,000	942,250

Monthly operating statement

	Flexed Budget	Actual	Variance Fav/(Adv)
Volume	110,000		
	£	£	£
Revenue		2,255,000	
Costs			
Material		425,000	
Labour		149,000	
Distribution		12,500	
Energy		110,250	
Equipment hire		32,000	
Depreciation		148,000	
Marketing		255,000	
Administration		181,000	
Total		1,312,750	
Operating profit		942,250	

Enter adverse variances as minus

Notes:

Material, labour and distribution costs are variable.

The budget for energy is semi-variable. The variable element is £0.80 per unit.

The budget for equipment hire is stepped, increasing at every 25,000 units of monthly production.

Depreciation, marketing and administration costs are fixed.

BACKWARDS VARIANCES CALCULATIONS

96 SALFORD

Salford Co's management accountant is investigating a favourable material price variance of £416 for 2016.

In 2016, 520 litres of Liquid A were purchased and used in manufacture and the actual cost of Liquid A was £4.50 per litre purchased.

What was the standard cost per litre purchased?

97 WINNIFRED

The table below is an extract from the budgeted variable costs to manufacture 300 units.

	Cost per unit £	Budgeted cost £
Materials	70	21,000

Actual production for the period was 260 units.

The total material variance was £780 adverse.

During the period, the actual cost of the material was £20 per kg and the standard quantity per unit was 5kgs.

Complete the table below:

Materials	**£**
Actual material cost	
Material price variance	
Material usage variance	
Standard material cost of production	

Section 2

ANSWERS TO PRACTICE QUESTIONS

SOURCES OF INFORMATION

Key answer tips

Make sure you read all the possible options in the 'Sources' column before making your decision.

1 SOURCES (I)

Data	Source
UK interest rates	Bank of England
Competitor prices	Pricing research
UK Economic growth forecasts	UK Treasury, independent economics consultants

2 SOURCES (II)

Data	Source
UK tax rates	HMRC publications
UK house prices	Building society data
Customer tastes	Market research

3 SOURCES (III)

Data	Source
French tax rates	French government
Political party likely to win power	Opinion poll surveys
Customer preferences	Market research

4 SOURCES (IV)

Data	Source
UK economic growth forecasts	UK treasury, independent economics consultants
UK duty rates (tax on alcohol etc.)	HMRC publications
Brazilian import tax rates	Brazilian government

BUDGETARY RESPONSIBILITIES

Key answer tips

Make sure you read all the possible options in the 'Contact' column before making your decision.

5 CONTACTS (I)

Situation	Contact
You want to identify any production constraints	Production planning manager
You want to forecast the cost of labour	Trade union representative
The budget is ready for final approval	Board of directors

6 CONTACTS (II)

Situation	Contact
You want to know the future strategy of the firm	Board of directors
You want to forecast the cost of machinery	Machinery buyers
You want to assess the efficiency of labour	Management accountants

Tutorial note

Any strategic element will involve the Board of Directors of a company.

7 CONTACTS (III)

Situation	Contact
You want to know day to day regional firm policy	Regional manager
You want to forecast sales	Sales team
You want to know idle time last period	Management accountants

8 CONTACTS (IV)

Situation	Contact
You want to forecast the price of raw materials	Firms' buying department
You want to examine competitors' prices	Other firms' price lists
You want to check the availability of skilled labour	Employment agency

9   THE RIGHT BUDGET

Capital expenditure	Marketing
New machinery	Magazine advertising
New delivery van	Incentives paid to sales staff

Maintenance
Spare parts for production machines
Salaries of repair engineers

Personnel	Cost of production
Salary of HR Manager	Wages of assembly line workers
	Raw material usage

10   CUMIN COMPANY

Resource Budget – Material X	Unit	December
Needed for production	kg	5,000
Wastage	kg	102
Total requirement	kg	5,102
Closing inventory	kg	950
Opening inventory	kg	900
Purchases in month	kg	5,152
Cost per kg	£	1
Purchase cost of material X	£	5152.04

11   DRAG AND DROP

Capital expenditure	Marketing
New conveyor belt	Television advertising
Enhancements to production machines	Commissions paid to sales staff

IT
Salary of IT manager
Wages of IT engineers

Personnel	Cost of production
Salary of HR Manager	Wages of production line workers

12   ADAM

Capital expenditure
New photocopier
New cars
New building

Marketing
Radio advertising
Market research costs
Internet advertising
Bonuses paid to sales team

Maintenance
Spare parts for production machines
Cost of machinery repairs
Spare parts for old trucks

Personnel
Salary of HR manager
Cost of HR staff

Cost of production
Lighting costs for factory
Raw material usage
Wages of assembly line workers
Cost of heating factory

ACCOUNTING TREATMENT OF OVERHEADS

13   ACCOUNTING TREATMENT (I)

• Materials used in the production process	Direct cost
• Administrative wages	Allocate to administrative overheads
• Depreciation of production equipment	Charge to production in a machine hour overhead rate
• Advertising costs	Allocate to marketing overheads
• Rent of a labour intensive production facility	Charge to production in a labour hour overhead rate
• Office stationery	Allocate to administrative overheads
• Idle time pay for production workers	Charge to production in a labour hour overhead rate
• Overtime premium for production workers	Charge to production in a labour hour overhead rate

14   ACCOUNTING TREATMENT (II)

• Materials used in the production process	Direct cost
• Rent of a machine intensive production facility	Charge to production in a machine hour overhead rate
• Office paper	Allocate to administrative overheads
• Basic pay for production workers	Direct cost
• Secretarial wages	Allocate to administrative overheads
• Overtime premium for production workers	Charge to production in a labour hour overhead rate
• Payments to marketing staff	Allocate to marketing overheads

15 ACCOUNTING TREATMENT (III)

• Wood used in the production process	Direct cost
• General postage costs	Allocate to administrative overheads
• Internet advertising costs	Allocate to marketing overheads
• Office stationery	Allocate to administrative overheads
• Chemicals used in the production process	Direct cost
• Idle time pay for production workers	Charge to production in a labour hour overhead rate
• Power costs for machinery	Charge to production in a machine hour overhead rate

INDICES

16 TACO

Sales revenue	Actual Year 1 £	Forecast Year 2 £	Forecast Year 3 £	Forecast Year 4 £	Forecast Year 5 £
At Year 1 prices	120,000	122,400	128,400	128,400	129,600
At expected prices		123,513	130,735	131,902	135,491

17 ARCHER

Sales revenue	Actual Year 1 £	Forecast Year 2 £	Forecast Year 3 £	Forecast Year 4 £	Forecast Year 5 £
At Year 1 prices	275,000	277,292	279,583	281,875	284,167
At expected prices		284,719	299,554	314,593	329,836

18 FLASH

Sales revenue	Actual Year 1 £	Forecast Year 2 £	Forecast Year 3 £	Forecast Year 4 £	Forecast Year 5 £
At Year 1 prices	280,000	287,119	289,492	291,864	294,237
At expected prices		294,809	310,169	325,742	341,525

19 SOPHIE

Sales revenue	Actual Year 1 £	Forecast Year 2 £	Forecast Year 3 £	Forecast Year 4 £	Forecast Year 5 £
At Year 1 prices	280,000	284,746	296,610	301,356	303,729
At expected prices		292,373	317,797	336,335	352,542

PRODUCTION BUDGETS

20 TITANIA

Production (units)	Week 1	Week 2	Week 3	Week 4	Week 5
Opening inventory	20,000	19,800	20,100	21,000	
Good production	64,800	66,300	67,900	70,600	
Sales Volume	65,000	66,000	67,000	70,000	72,000
Closing inventory	19,800	20,100	21,000	21,600	

	Week 1	Week 2	Week 3	Week 4
Rejected Production	2,005	2,051	2,100	2,184
Total manufactured units	66,805	68,351	70,000	72,784

Tutorial note

There are different ways of going about this, and you must find the approach that works best for you. For example, the following method could be applied to tackle this task.

*First, fill in the 'Closing Inventory' row. You are told in the question that **'Closing inventory should be 30% of the following week's sales volume'**. So in week 1, closing inventory is 30% of Week 2 sales volume; this means 30% of 66,000 = 19,800. In week 2, closing inventory is 30% of Week 3 sales volume; this means 30% of 67,000 = 20,100. Fill in all four values like this.*

Secondly, rewrite all these values you have just calculated for closing inventory as 'opening inventory' for the following week. So closing inventory for week 1 (19800) becomes the opening inventory for week 2. Closing inventory for week 2 (20100) becomes the opening inventory for week 3. Closing inventory for week 3 (21000) becomes the opening inventory for week 4.

Thirdly, calculate the good production for week 1. Good production is equal to the sales volume units PLUS the closing inventory units, but LESS the units that were already there to start the week i.e. the opening inventory units. So, for week 1, we calculate 'Good production' as Sales volume 65,000 units + Closing Inventory 19800 units – opening inventory units 20,000 = 64,800 units. Repeat this for every week.

*In the second table, that contains the 'Rejected production' and 'Total manufactured units' rows, you should start with your 'Total manufactured units' answer. The total number of manufactured units represents 100% of the total production. The 'Good Production' you had calculated before (64,800 units) only represents 97% of the total production, as 3% of the total production was faulty. So by dividing 64,800 units by 97, you get 1% of total production, i.e. 668.04 units. Leave this number in you calculator and multiply it by 100: this is your total production of **66,805** units (rounded up). The last number to fill in is that for rejected production, which is always your total production **(66,805)** less your good production of 64800 units = 2,005. Repeat the same approach for every week in the table.*

21   PUCK

Production (units)	Week 1	Week 2	Week 3	Week 4	Week 5
Opening inventory	35,000	23,400	23,400	21,000	
Good production	68,400	78,000	75,600	73,000	
Sales Volume	80,000	78,000	78,000	70,000	80,000
Closing inventory	23,400	23,400	21,000	24,000	

	Week 1	Week 2	Week 3	Week 4	
Rejected Production	2,850	3,250	3,150	3,042	
Total manufactured units	71,250	81,250	78,750	76,042	

22   OBERON

Production (units)	Week 1	Week 2	Week 3	Week 4	Week 5
Opening inventory	32,000	23,400	22,500	21,000	
Good production	69,400	77,100	73,500	73,000	
Sales Volume	78,000	78,000	75,000	70,000	80,000
Closing inventory	23,400	22,500	21,000	24,000	

	Week 1	Week 2	Week 3	Week 4	
Rejected Production	7,712	8,567	8,167	8,112	
Total manufactured units	77,112	85,667	81,667	81,112	

23   LYSANDER

Production (units)	Week 1	Week 2	Week 3	Week 4	Week 5
Opening inventory	20,000	19,500	20,100	21,000	
Good production	64,500	65,600	67,900	70,600	
Sales Volume	65,000	65,000	67,000	70,000	72,000
Closing inventory	19,500	20,100	21,000	21,600	

	Week 1	Week 2	Week 3	Week 4	
Rejected Production	1,317	1,339	1,386	1,441	
Total manufactured units	65,817	66,939	69,286	72,041	

24   DEMETRIUS

Production (units)	Week 1	Week 2	Week 3	Week 4	Week 5
Opening inventory	19,000	19,800	20,100	21,000	
Good production	65,800	66,300	67,900	70,600	
Sales Volume	65,000	66,000	67,000	70,000	72,000
Closing inventory	19,800	20,100	21,000	21,600	

	Week 1	Week 2	Week 3	Week 4	
Rejected Production	1,343	1,354	1,386	1,441	
Total manufactured units	67,143	67,654	69,286	72,041	

25 HERMIA

Production (units)	Week 1	Week 2	Week 3	Week 4	Week 5
Opening inventory	19,000	19,800	20,100	21,000	
Good production	65,800	66,300	67,900	73,000	
Sales Volume	65,000	66,000	67,000	70,000	80,000
Closing inventory	19,800	20,100	21,000	24,000	

	Week 1	Week 2	Week 3	Week 4	Week 5
Rejected Production	2,036	2,051	2,100	2,258	2,035
Total manufactured units	67,836	68,351	70,000	75,258	67,835

26 EVIE

Units of product A	Week 1	Week 2	Week 3	Week 4	Week 5
Opening inventory	1,000	2,000	1,875	1,750	2,000
Production	8,000	7,875	7,375	7,250	
Sub-total	9,000	9,875	9,250	9,000	
Sales	7,000	8,000	7,500	7,000	8,000
Closing inventory	2,000	1,875	1,750	2,000	

27 EGO

Units of Ego	Week 1	Week 2	Week 3	Week 4	Week 5
Opening inventory	2,000	4,000	3,750	3,500	4,000
Production	16,000	15,750	14,750	14,500	
Sub-total	18,000	19,750	18,500	18,000	
Sales	14,000	16,000	15,000	14,000	16,000
Closing inventory	4,000	3,750	3,500	4,000	

28 PRODUCT C

Units of product C	Week 1	Week 2	Week 3	Week 4	Week 5
Opening inventory	500	800	750	700	800
Production	3,800	3,950	3,700	3,600	
Sub-total	4,300	4,750	4,450	4,300	
Sales	3,500	4,000	3,750	3,500	4,000
Closing inventory	800	750	700	800	

29 PRODUCT B

	Month 1	Month 2	Month 3
Required units	90,250	95,000	99,750
Manufactured units	95,000	100,000	105,000

30   ROPE

	Month 1	Month 2	Month 3
Required units	180,670	190,980	185,900
Manufactured units	190,179	201,032	195,685

31   CAMELIA

Tutorial note

There are different ways of getting to the right answer but make sure you do not confuse minutes with hours in your calculations.

800 hours of overtime.

Working:

104,000 × 3/60 = 5,200 hrs required.

5,200 − (25 × 176) = 800 hrs overtime needed.

32   SAGE

66,500m

Working:

20,000 items @ 2.5 metres = 50,000 metres.

50,000m × 100/80 (wastage) = 62,500m

Plus 14,000m closing stock less 10,000m = 66,500m

33   BUMBLEBEE

Tutorial note

Remember to round up to the nearest whole unit.

	Month 1	Month 2	Month 3
Required units	18,900	20,150	22,200
Manufactured units	19,286	20,562	22,654

34   QUALITY CONTROL

There is labour available to make **231,000** units in normal time. Therefore, **13,500** hours of overtime will be needed.

The raw material contract will provide enough material to make **200,000** units. Therefore, **100,000** kg will have to be purchased on the open market.

Quality control can test **216,000** units in the year. It will be necessary to make alternative arrangements for **24,000** units.

35   COMPANY A

There is labour available to make **131,250** units in normal time. Therefore, **10,500** hours of overtime will be needed.

The raw material contract will provide enough material to make **100,000** units. Therefore, **72,000** kg will have to be purchased on the open market.

Quality control can test **120,000** units in the year. It will be necessary to make alternative arrangements for **20,000** units.

36   JONES

There is labour available to make **131,250** units in normal time. Therefore, **15,000** hours of overtime will be needed.

The raw material contract will provide enough material to make **100,000** units. Therefore, **150,000** kg will have to be purchased on the open market.

Quality control can test **144,000** units in the year. It will be necessary to make alternative arrangements for **6,000** units.

37   DONALD

200

Working:

$84,000 \times 3/60 = 4,200$ hrs basic time.

$4,200 - (25 \times 160) = 200$ hrs overtime.

38   THEO

40

Working:

$48,000 \times 6/60 = 4,800$ hrs required.

$4,800 - (28 \times 170) = 40$ hrs overtime needed.

MACHINE UTILISATION

39   E, F AND G

Product	Units	Hours per unit	Hours required
E	100	1.0	100
F	230	2.0	460
G	370	3.5	1,295
Total hours for Department Y			1,855

How many additional machines should be hired?   3

40   ZEE

Product	Units	Hours per unit	Hours required
C	200	0.5	100
D	460	2.0	920
E	740	2.5	1,850
Total hours for Zee			2,870

How many additional machines should be hired?   1

41   CLAUDIO

Tutorial note

The total number of machine hours available is 100 machines × 80 hours each = 8,000 hours.

For each product A, B and C, hours required = Items × hours per item:

- *For A, hours required = 2,000 items × 1.00 hour per item = 2,000 hours.*

- *For B, hours required = 1,750 items × 2.00 hours per item = 3,500 hours.*

- *For C, hours required = 610 items × 3.00 hours per item = 1,830 hours.*

We have calculated in the above table that the total machine hours required (sum of hours required for products A, B and C) is 7,330 hours.

This represents (7,330 hours/8,000 hours) × 100 = 91.625% of the total number of hours available (we round up to 92%).

Budgeted machine loading	Items	Hours per item	Hours required
Product			
A	2,000	1.00	2,000
B	1,750	2.00	3,500
C	610	3.00	1,830
Total machine hours required			7,330
% utilisation			92%

42   DOGBERRY

Budgeted machine loading	Items	Hours per item	Hours required
Product			
A	120	3.75	450
B	175	1.50	263
C	190	1.50	285
Total machine hours required			998
% utilisation			40%

43   LEONATO

Budgeted machine loading	Items	Hours per item	Hours required
Product			
A	250	3.00	750
B	1,000	1.00	1,000
C	390	1.50	585
Total machine hours required			2,335
% utilisation			98%

44   BORACHIO

Budgeted machine loading	Items	Hours per item	Hours required
Product			
A	25	4	100
B	10	2	20
C	40	1.50	60
Total machine hours required			180
% utilisation			90%

CAPACITY CONSTRAINTS

45 GLOUCESTER

Tutorial note

From the question, we have 2,500 kilograms of materials available. As every unit requires 1 kilogram, we therefore have sufficient materials to manufacture 2,500 kilograms/ 1 kilogram per unit = 2,500 units.

420 hours of direct labour available represent 420 × 60 minutes = 25,200 minutes; that is sufficient to produce (before overtime is needed) (25,200/40 minutes of labour per unit) = 630 units.

120 hours of machine time represent 120 × 60 minutes = 7,200 minutes, which is sufficient to produce 7,200/5 minutes per hour = 1,440 units.

Without overtime, the maximum sales volume is (as labour is the limiting factor) 630 units.

With unlimited overtime, the maximum overtime is (as labour is no longer a limiting factor) 1440 units (as machine time becomes the limiting factor then).

Production capacity	Units
Sufficient materials are budgeted to manufacture	2,500
Without overtime, sufficient direct labour is budgeted to manufacture	630
Sufficient machine time is budgeted to manufacture	1,440
Without overtime, the maximum sales volume is	630
With unlimited overtime, the maximum sales volume is	1,440

46 BEDFORD

Production capacity	Units
Sufficient materials are budgeted to manufacture	100
Without overtime, sufficient direct labour is budgeted to manufacture	300
Sufficient machine time is budgeted to manufacture	432
Without overtime, the maximum sales volume is	100
With unlimited overtime, the maximum sales volume is	100

WORKING SCHEDULES AND OPERATING BUDGETS

47   WASHINGTON

Materials	Kg	£
Opening inventory	2,200	3,080
Purchases @ £1.50 per kg	82,800	124,200
Sub-total	85,000	127,280
Used	50,000	74,780
Closing inventory	35,000	52,500
Closing inventory to be valued at budgeted purchase price		

Labour	Hours	£
Basic time @ £16 per hour	1,600	25,600
Overtime	400	9,600
Total	2,000	35,200

Production Overhead	Hours	£
Variable @ £2.50 per hour	2,000	5,000
Fixed		165,020
Total		170,020

48   ADAMS

Operating budget	Units	£ per unit	£
Sales revenue	18,000	27.00	486,000

Cost of goods sold		£
Opening inventory of finished goods		40,000
Cost of production	£	
Materials	74,780	
Labour	35,200	
Production overhead	170,020	280,000
Closing inventory of finished goods		42,700
Cost of goods sold		277,300
Gross profit/(loss)		208,700
Overheads	£	
Administration	80,000	
Marketing	25,000	105,000
Operating profit/(loss)		103,700

49   JEFFERSON

Materials	Kg	£
Opening inventory	20,000	12,000
Purchases @ £2.00 per kg	97,500	195,000
Sub-total	117,500	207,000
Used	82,500	137,000
Closing inventory	35,000	70,000
Closing inventory to be valued at budgeted purchase price		

Labour	Hours	£
Basic time @ £8.00 per hour	2,100	16,800
Overtime	1,200	14,400
Total	3,300	31,200

Production Overheads	Hours	£
Variable @ £2.00 per hour	3,300	6,600
Fixed		155,200
Total		161,800

50   BURR

Operating budget	Units	£ per unit	£
Sales revenue	15,000	30.00	450,000
Cost of goods sold			£
Opening inventory of finished goods			40,000
Cost of production		£	
Materials		137,000	
Labour		31,200	
Production overhead		161,800	330,000
Closing inventory of finished goods			90,000
Cost of goods sold			280,000
Gross profit/(loss)			170,000
Overheads		£	
Administration		55,000	
Marketing		60,000	115,000
Operating profit/(loss)			55,000

51   JUNEAU

1   (a)   Production budget (units)

		Key	Jet
Sales		9,350	10,120
Add	Closing finished stocks	1,353	2,585
Less	Opening finished stocks	(1,103)	(1,305)
Planned production		9,600	11,400

Closing stocks: Key: 11,275 × 3/25 and Jet: 12,925 × 5/25

(b)   Materials purchase budget (kilograms)

Production Keys: 9,600 × 11	105,600
Production Jets: 11,400 × 14	159,600
	265,200
Wastage: 265,200 × 3/97	8,202.06
Purchases (kg)	273,403

Tutorial note

We chose to round up to 273,403 kgs here to ensure sufficient purchases are made for production.

(c)   Cost of material purchases budget

273,403 × £6	£1,640,418

(d)   Direct hours labour budget

Key:	9,600/8	1,200
Jet:	11,400/4	2,850
		4,050
Basic hours available:	23 × 35 × 5	4,025
Overtime		25

(e)   Cost of labour budget

Total direct labour hours	4,050 × £8	£32,400
Alternative answer 1:		
Basic hours	4,025 × £8	£32,200
Overtime	25 × £8	£200
		£32,400
Alternative answer 2:		
Actual hours	Key: 1,200 × £8	9,600
	Jet: 2,850 × £8	22,800
		£32,400

(f)   Total absorption cost of production

	Key	Jet
Materials	653,196	987,216
Labour	9,600	22,800
Overheads	18,000	42,750
	680,796	1,052,766

Material:	Key	[9,600 × 11] × [100/97] × £6
	Jet	[11,400 × 14] × [100/97] × £6
Labour:	Key	1,200 × £8
	Jet	2,850 × £8
Overheads:	Key	1,200 × £15
	Jet	2,850 × £15

(g)   Absorption cost of opening finished stocks

(i)   Key: 1,103 × £51 = £56,253

(ii)   Jet: 1,305 × £66 = £86,130

MEMO

To:	Axel Dell	**From:**	Management accountant
Subject:	Additional production	**Date:**	15 June 2010

This report has been prepared in response to the request to produce additional amounts of 2,000 Keys and 2,000 Jets in Period 11. Using the information supplied, the increased planned production is set out below. This has been considered from the possibility of either labour or materials being a constraint on achieving the required extra amounts.

Calculations of possible constraints

(a) (i) Labour

	Key	Jet	Total
Units planned	9,600	11,400	
Direct labour hours required	1,200	2,850	4050
Hours required for increased production			
Keys: 2,000/8	250		
Jets: 2,000/4		500	750
Total hours required			4,800
Revised hours:			
Standard hours available (23 − 3) × 35 × 5			3,500
Maximum overtime 20 × 60			1,200
Shortfall in hours required			(100)

(ii) **Materials**

Additional production required (rounded up)			
2,000 × 11 kg × 100/97	22,681		
2,000 × 14 kg × 100/97		28,866	51,547
Additional materials available			52,000
Excess material available			453

(b) **Revised production budget**

From these calculations, it can be seen that labour is the effective constraint. Consequently, it will only be possible to produce the following number of Keys and Jets in Period 7.

This is just one option – it would be equally valid to reduce one product only in line with maximising *highest contribution per unit for example.*

	Key	Jet
Original production + additional required	11,600	13,400
Additional production limited by		
Keys (100 × 2,000/4,000) = 50 × 8	(400)	
Jets (100 × 2,000/4,000) = 50 × 4		(200)
Total revised production	11,200	13,200

(c) **Suggested recommendations to overcome the restriction**

- employ temporary staff to cover the sickness absences
- allow extra overtime.

52 SINCLAIR LTD

1 **(a)** **Production budget – 4 periods to 21 October 2011**

	1	2	3	4	5 (*)
Sales volume	19,400	21,340	23,280	22,310	22,310
Add: closing inventory	4,268	4,656	4,462	4,462	
Less opening inventory	(3,880)	(4,268)	(4,656)	(4,462)	(4,462)
Good production	19,788	21,728	23,086	22,310	
Faulty production (3/97)	612	672	714	690	
Gross production of Doms	20,400	22,400	23,800	23,000	

Notes:

Closing Inventory = 4/20 × next period's sales volumes.

Closing Inventory equals next period's opening inventory.

(*) Period 5 shown to demonstrate calculation of period 4's closing inventory.

(b) **Material purchases budget – 3 periods to 23 September 2011**

	1	2	3	4
Gross production of Doms	20,400	22,400	23,800	23,000
Material required (3 litres per Dom)	61,200	67,200	71,400	69,000
Add closing inventory	16,800	17,850	17,250	
Less opening inventory	(16,500)	(16,800)	(17,850)	(17,250)
Purchases, in litres	61,500	68,250	70,800	

(c)   Cost of purchases

	1	2	3
Purchases, in litres	61,500	68,250	70,800
Cost £8	£8	£8	£8
Total cost in £	492,000	546,000	566,400

(d)   Labour budget – 3 periods to 23 September 2011

	1	2	3
Gross production of Doms	20,400	22,400	23,800
Hours (0.5 hours per Dom)	10,200	11,200	11,900
Basic hours (70 workers × 40 hours × 4 weeks)	11,200	11,200	11,200
Overtime (surplus hours)	(1,000)	NIL	700

(e)   Cost of wages

	1	2	3
Basic wages (70 workers × 4 weeks × £240)	£67,200	£67,200	£67,200
Overtime (£9 × overtime hours)			£6,300
	£67,200	£67,200	£73,500

2

MEMO

To: Production director

From: Management accountant

Date: XX June 2001

Subject: Overtime payments and faulty production

Following our recent meeting to discuss the budgets, you questioned the need for over-time and made the observation that the 3% failure rate may be due to poor working practices on the shop floor.

(a)   **Overtime payments**

There are 700 hours of overtime allowed for in the budget during period 3. There is however a surplus of labour capacity of 1,000 hours in period 1. If we produce an extra 1,400 units in period 1, the overtime hours in period 3 would be avoided.

This would result in a saving of (£9 × 700 hours) = £6,300.

(b)   **Costs incurred in achieving the overtime saving (one only required)**

- Financing costs
- Storage costs.

CASH FLOW FORECASTS

53 WASHINGTON AND ADAMS

Tutorial note

'Sales receipts' is not the same as 'Sales revenue' because even if we have made a sale, it doesn't necessarily mean that we have received the cash for that sale. We need to look at the 'Receivables' movement and this information is given to us in the requirement. Here, we are told that 'Receivables' are expected to decrease by £162,000 over the year. This means that, as well as receiving cash from sales of £486,000 as we calculated in the 'Adams' question, we also have received £162,000 from our debtors.

Therefore, 'Total sales receipts' = £486,000 + £162000 = £648,000.

- *'Payments for materials': the expenditure in the 'Washington' schedule for materials stands at £124,200, but this is not necessarily the amount that has been paid to our suppliers/ creditors in cash. Balance Sheet movements tell us that our creditors (='Payables') will increase by £26,800 over the year, which is decreasing the level of cash paid and increasing our debt to creditors. Therefore, amount of cash paid is £124,200 – £26,800 = £97,400.*

- *'Payments for labour' is straightforward, and can be copied down from 'Washington' or 'Adams' a value of £35,200.*

- *As depreciation is not a cash flow, the depreciation charge of £19,000 must be taken away from the total production overheads of £170,020 calculated in 'Adams', so*

- *Production overhead cash flows = £170,020 – £19,000 = £151,020.*

- *'Other overheads' represent the addition of the marketing and admin overheads given to us in 'Adams' : £80,000 + £25,000 = £105,000.*

Cash flow forecast	£	
Opening cash balance/(overdraft)		29,650
Sales receipts		648,000
Payments		
Materials	97,400	
Labour	35,200	
Production overhead	151,020	
Other overheads	105,000	
Capital expenditure	50,000	438,620
Closing cash balance/(overdraft)		239,030

54 JEFFERSON AND BURR

Tutorial note

'Payments for materials': in this example, our creditors (= 'Payables') will decrease by £32,600 over the year, which is increasing the level of cash paid and decreasing our debt to creditors.

Cash flow forecast	£	
Opening cash balance/(overdraft)		90,000
Sales receipts		465,000
Payments		
Materials	227,600	
Labour	31,200	
Production overhead	146,800	
Other overheads	115,000	
Capital expenditure	120,000	640,600
Closing cash balance/(overdraft)		−85,600

55 CASH FORECAST FOR MAY

Cash forecast	May
	£
Opening cash balance	−320
Customer receipts	7,810
Payments	
For purchases	6,700
For wages	400
For overheads	540
For capital exp.	0
Total	7,640
Closing cash balance	−150

56 THE LATEST

Cash-flow forecast	£	£
Sales receipts		262,000
Payments		
Materials	111,200	
Labour	41,250	
Other costs	14,400	166,850
Cash-flow forecast		95,150

57 HARVEST FESTIVAL

Cash-flow forecast	£	£
Sales receipts		113,500
Payments		
Materials	32,500	
Labour	26,200	
Other costs	17,350	76,050
Cash-flow forecast		37,450

58 OKTOBERFEST

Cash flow forecast	£	£
Sales receipts		156,800
Payments		
Materials	55,550	
Labour	20,000	
Other costs	22,450	98,000
Cash Flow forecast		58,800

PERIODIC BUDGETS

59 APRIL BUDGETS

	Budget for the year	Budget for April
Units sold	34,000	3,000
Units produced	36,000	3,500

		£
Sales	204,000	18,000
Materials used	59,400	5,775
Labour	67,200	6,800
Variable production overhead	54,000	5,250
Fixed overhead	3,600	300

Working:

Budgeted annual labour hours = 36,000 × 6 mins ÷ 60 = 3,600 hours

Standard variable overhead rate per hour = £54,000/3,600 = £15/hr

April labour hours = 3,500 × 6/60 = 350 hours

April variable overhead = 350 × 15 = £5,250

60   ROSE

	Budget for the year	Budget for May
Units sold	68,000	6,000
Units produced	72,000	7,000
	£	£
Sales	1,408,000	124,235
Materials used	720,000	70,000
Labour	264,000	27,000
Variable production overhead	96,000	9,333
Fixed overhead	3,600	300

Working:

Budgeted annual labour hours = 72,000 × 10 mins ÷ 60 = 12,000 hours

Standard variable overhead rate per hour = £96,000/12,000 = £8/hr

May labour hours = 7,000 × 10/60 = 1166.67 hours

May variable overhead = 1166.67 × 8 = £9,333

61   SALES AND COSTS

	Budget for the year	Budget for June
Units sold	120,000	11,000
Units produced	110,000	10,000
	£	£
Sales	1,649,000	151,158
Materials used	1,155,000	105,000
Labour	95,500	9,000
Variable production overhead	55,000	5,000
Fixed overhead	3,600	300

ALTERNATIVE SCENARIOS

62   MADISON

Operating budget	First draft	Alternative scenario
Sales price per unit (£)	15.00	15.75
Sales volume	75,000	69,000
		£
Sales revenue	1,125,000	1,086,750
Costs		
Material	131,250	120,750
Labour	187,500	172,500
Energy	44,000	43,200
Depreciation	62,400	56,160
Total	425,150	392,610
Gross Profit	699,850	694,140
Increase/(decrease) in gross profit		–5,710

Tutorial note

First, you can calculate a selling price increase from £15.00 to £15.00 × (1 + 5%) = £15.75.

The decrease in sales volume can be calculated as 75,000 units in the first draft × (1–8%) = 69,000 units. By multiplying these two numbers together, we then get sales revenue in the alternative scenario of £1,086,750.

Material costs are variable, as we are told in the question. With the first draft numbers we can calculate that the material cost per unit is £131,250/75,000 units, i.e. £1.75 per unit. We apply this to the alternative scenario volumes of 69,000 units and get a new material cost of £120,750.

Likewise, labour costs are variable, as we are told in the question. With the first draft numbers we can calculate that the labour cost per unit is £187,500/75,000 units, i.e. £2.50 per unit. We apply this to the alternative scenario volumes of 69,000 units and get a new labour cost of £172,500.

In the first draft, energy costs currently stand at £44,000. This £44,000 amount includes a rise of 10%. Before this rise of 10% was incorporated in the calculation, we had an energy cost of £44,000/(1-10%), i.e. £44,000/90% so £40,000. In the alternative scenario we may then increase this starting amount of £40,000 by the revised increase of 8% and get a new energy cost of £40,000 × (1 + 8%) = £43,200.

Depreciation is the trickiest number to calculate in this task. It is a stepped cost and in the first draft we had 75,000 units/8,000 units = 9.375 steps of 8,000 units. We must round this up to 10 steps. If 10 steps incurred a depreciation expense of £62,400 in the first draft, it means that each 'step' incurs a depreciation expense of £62,400/10 steps = £6,240. So, in the alternative scenario where we have 69,000 units, we have 69,000 units/8,000 units per step = 8.625 steps. We must round this up to 9 steps, and 9 × £6,240 = £56,160.

63   MONROE

Operating budget	First draft	Alternative scenario
Sales price per unit (£)	20.00	21.00
Sales volume	6,200	6,076
		£
Sales revenue	124,000	127,596
Costs		
Material	4,650	4,557
Labour	12,400	12,152
Energy	33,000	30,900
Depreciation	14,000	14,000
Total	64,050	61,609
Gross Profit	59,950	65,987
Increase/(decrease) in gross profit		6,037

SALES REVENUE AND COSTS FORECASTS

64   INCOME FORECAST (I)

Tutorial note

When deflating a revenue (i.e. stripping the effect of inflation on forecasts), ensure you divide (not multiply) the inflated number with the increase percentage given in the question.

$$\frac{£4,284,000 \text{ forecast for next year, including 2\% increase}}{1+2\% \text{ increase}} = £4,200,000$$

65   INCOME FORECAST (II)

The forecast should be revised to **£7,200,000**

66   INCOME FORECAST (III)

The forecast should be revised to **£800,000**

67   ENERGY COSTS

The energy budget should be **£143,820**

68 ELECTRICITY COSTS

The energy budget should be **£197,600**

$$\frac{\text{£212,160 forecast for next year, including 2\% increase}}{1+2\% \text{ increase}} = \text{£208,000 before the increase.}$$

After the reduction, we have £208,000 × (1 − 5%) = £197,600.

The 4% increase in gas and electricity tariffs remains and no changes in calculations are needed.

69 FORECASTS

Quarter	£
1	585,000
2	570,000
3	540,000
4	505,000
Year	2,200,000

70 FLUTE

Quarter	£
1	1,230,000
2	1,250,000
3	1,335,000
4	985,000
Year	4,800,000

SAMPLING

71 STRATIFIED SAMPLING

Age range	Up to 29	30 to 39	40 to 49	Over 49	Total
Number of customers	23,500	24,000	41,500	54,000	143,000
Sample	164	168	290	378	1,000

72 HOURS IN A DAY

Age range	Up to 29	30 to 39	40 to 49	Over 49	Total
Number of customers	69,500	57,000	42,500	12,200	181,200
Sample	767	629	469	135	2,000

73 PARIS KITCHEN

Age range	Up to 29	30 to 39	40 to 49	Over 49	Total
Number of customers	25,500	32,000	42,000	54,000	153,500
Sample	17	21	27	35	100

74 RACHEL

Age range	Up to 29	30 to 39	40 to 49	Over 49	Total
Number of customers	1,300	5,900	5,700	5,000	17,900
Sample	18	82	80	70	250

75 SAMPLING ARMISTICE

Age range	Up to 29	30 to 39	40 to 49	Over 49	Total
Number of customers	16,000	22,000	45,000	20,000	103,000
Sample	233	320	655	291	1,500

76 ADVENT

Age range	Up to 29	30 to 39	40 to 49	Over 49	Total
Number of customers	15,000	15,500	15,000	15,600	61,100
Sample	614	634	614	638	2,500

WRITTEN EMAIL TASKS

77   NOSEY

To	Chief executive	**Date**	(Today)
From	Budget accountant	**Subject**	Review of operating statement

(a)   Reasons for variances

I have reviewed the results for May 2009. Profit in the month was £1,933,900 driven by a 10% price improvement over budget and increased volume. After flexing the original budget to allow for the increased volume we are reporting adverse expense variances of £109,700.

The most significant adverse expense variance is labour. I would expect this cost variance to be adverse because increased workloads tend to create high overtime costs and this appears to be the case here.

Material costs were above budget despite the reduction in the chemical costs during the month. We need to investigate whether working overtime has resulted in the staff being tired which may have led to higher levels of material wastage. It may be preferable to employ additional staff instead.

Marketing costs were £16,800 over budget, no doubt due to the costs of the advertising campaign, and this seems to be money well spent.

The administration overspend is worrying and needs to be investigated. It could have been a one-off. Alternatively, perhaps there are variable costs such as overtime or bonus that should not have been budgeted as fixed costs.

(b)   Three steps to motivate managers to achieve budgets

Maintaining motivated managers is an important aspect of setting and achieving budgets.

To do this, managers should be involved in the planning process so that budgets are not set at unachievable levels.

Proper lines of communication should be established so that managers can be kept informed and understand the part they have to play in achieving the budgets.

The establishment of performance targets that are challenging and lead to acceptable rewards, such as salary increases or bonuses, is another way of keeping managers motivated.

78   CM LTD

To	Chief executive	Date	(Today)
From	Budget accountant	Subject	Review of operating statement

(a)   Examine the planning assumptions and calculations in the proposed budget and identify any weaknesses.

The draft budget is based on the assumption of 10% growth in sales volume. No justification is offered for this round figure assumption. I suggest that we need to review recent trends in CM Ltd's products; look at the potential for the anticipated new products and estimate the likely additional business generated from our own customers. With only 50 current products, this should not be difficult.

The assumption that sales revenue will only grow relative to sales volume is probably pessimistic. Although we are told prices can never be raised, new products should command a healthy margin when launched, particularly as they are patent protected.

All costs have been increased by 12.5% in the draft budget (2.5% for inflation and 10% for growth). There is no reason why fixed costs should increase by more than an appropriate rate for inflation. Each line of costs needs to be considered carefully according to its cost type (variable, fixed, etc.) and its own cost pressures.

In particular, agreement is required about the management bonus. This has been accrued at £21,000 for 2016 and, in effect, budgeted at £23,625 for 2017. This has not yet been approved.

(b)   Explain how costs and profitability should be managed in an organisation that manufactures multiple products.

In a multi-product manufacturing business, it is essential that costs and profitability are reviewed by product. Therefore, a costing system needs to be in place.

A standard costing system has particular advantages in that it is based on calculations of what the costs should be – called standard costs. This is useful for control as variances from these standards can be reported and investigated.

The standard cost of each product can be compared with its selling price to identify profitability.

Standard costs can be calculated for planned new products to inform price setting.

(c)   Give your opinion, with reasons, on how well the budget would motivate managers to create sustainable, profitable growth.

Budgetary control can be a powerful tool to encourage managers and staff to create sustainable, profitable growth. To do this, budgets need to be stretching but achievable.

The proposed CM Ltd budget has been prepared by its own directors who have a vested interest, in the form of the management bonus, in ensuring that it is easy to achieve. They have not provided sufficient supporting data to enable us to verify that the sales volume and pricing assumptions are stretching.

Increasing all costs, fixed and variable, by 12.5% cannot be justified and creates significant budgetary slack.

I do not believe that this draft budget would motivate CM Ltd to create sustainable, profitable growth.

79 CONTROLLABILITY

To	Chief executive	**Date**	(Today)
From	Assistant Management Accountant	**Subject**	Review of variances

(a)	**Performance of production manager and sales manager**

- The production manager Jon McRae seems to have been operating in a well performing department in February (before the move to cotton).

- In a traditional sense, the production manager has seriously overspent in March following the move to cotton. He has a net variance against his department of £3,200 in the month of March.

- The sales manager seems to have missed his targets in February, but the change to cotton certainly helped him achieve a huge favourable variance in March.

- The move to a better quality material (but more expensive) can partly or wholly explain the adverse material variance in March for Jon McRae, but a higher quality has certainly contributed to the increased sales of clothes (reflected in a favourable sales variance in March).

- The adverse material usage variance may be the result of more waste as the workers get used to using cotton rather than nylon.

(b)	**Controllability of variances in R&T and the fairness of the bonus scheme**

- No adjustment to the standards has been made between the two months to allow for the change to cotton.

- Variances have to be allocated to one individual. In R&T, the good sales variances have been allocated to the sales manager, when in truth, the Production Manager's decision to use cotton appears to have been the driver of business success.

- Under out-of-date standards, Jon Mc Rae has no chance of making a bonus as the price of cotton is totally out of his control.

- The system does not appear to be fair.

80   FRANKA

To	Chief executive	**Date**	(Today)
From	Budget accountant	**Subject**	Review of operating statement

> **(a)   Key variances and reasons for increase in the actual profit**
>
> There are three significant adverse variances, relating to revenue, materials and labour. The adverse variance on revenue shows that the actual selling price of the product was less than planned. In addition, it would appear that either the unit material and unit labour costs were greater than planned or the material usage and labour productivity were adverse compared to the budget.
>
> There are three favourable variances: power, depreciation and marketing. The reduced cost of electricity arose from decisions by the supplier and not from the introduction of performance-related pay. The favourable variance on marketing might not be in the company's best interest as demand may fall without advertising support. Finally, depreciation is a non-cash item and any change is more likely to reflect a policy change rather than any enhanced performance by senior managers. Hence the increase in actual profit is unlikely to be due to the introduction of performance-related pay.

> **(b)   FOUR general conditions necessary for performance-related pay to successfully lead to improved performance in organisations**
>
> 1   Budgets need to be consistent with the objectives of the whole organisation.
>
> 2   Managers must feel that the objectives are achievable but they should also provide a challenge.
>
> 3   The level of rewards – both financial and non-financial – should be sufficient to help motivate managers.
>
> 4   The actual results should not be capable of being manipulated.

81 LABOUR COSTS

To	Production director	**Date**	(Today)
From	Budget accountant	**Subject**	Direct labour budget

(a) **Budget submission**

I attach the proposed direct labour budget for next year for your consideration and approval.

The agreed production plan indicates an increase in volume to 1,650,000 units next year. No change in productivity has been assumed. Therefore the staffing level needs to increase by 23 to 81.

The manager of human resources estimates that average pay will increase by 5% next year to £31,500.

Please let me know if you need any further information.

(b) **Performance indicators**

There is a range of useful measures to monitor cost, efficiency, effectiveness and employee satisfaction. Staff hours and output data should be available on a daily basis. Labour rates are reviewed periodically. However employee satisfaction is probably best canvassed once or twice a year. I recommend that we conduct a weekly review of performance based on:

- Minutes per unit

- Hours of overtime

- Percentage of good output (or similar quality measure)

- Average hourly rate

We should also commission a confidential employee satisfaction and involvement questionnaire.

82 X AND Z

X Limited	Indicator	Indicator
Year	**2009**	**2008**
Operating profit margin	−23.33%	−8.18%
Interest cover	0	0
Current ratio	0.93	1.11

Z Limited	Indicator	Indicator
Year	**2009**	**2008**
Operating profit margin	14.44%	6.88%
Interest cover	5.2	2.2
Current ratio	1.53	1.54

83 DIEGO

To	Production director	Date	(Today)
From	Budget accountant	Subject	Direct labour budget

(a) Budget submission

I attach the proposed direct labour budget for next year for your consideration and approval.

As you know, the tough economic climate has impacted the company's sales and there is a need for productivity to increase as profits are squeezed.

The agreed production plan indicates a 21% decrease in volume to 950,000 units next year. An increase in productivity has been assumed as the minutes per unit should fall from 6 to 5.4. The increased productivity, the decreased production volume and an assumed increase in annual hours per staff member enables the staffing level to fall by 21 to 46.

The manager of human resources estimates that average pay will decrease by approximately 3% next year to £34,000.

Please let me know if you need any further information.

(b) Performance indicators

There is a range of useful measures to monitor how well the company is doing in financial terms. These include the calculation of:

- Net profit margin
- Gross profit margin
- Return on capital employed
- Asset turnover.

84 DRAFT BUDGET

To	Production director	Date	(Today)
From	Budget accountant	Subject	Direct labour budget

(a) Budget submission

I attach the proposed direct labour budget for next year for your consideration and approval.

The agreed production plan indicates an increase in volume to 1,500,000 units next year. An increase in productivity has been assumed. The staffing level needs to increase by 8 to 52.

The manager of human resources estimates that average pay will increase by approximately 6% next year to £36,000. This is due to labour shortages.

Please let me know if you need any further information.

(b) **Performance indicators**

There is a range of useful measures to monitor cost, efficiency, effectiveness and employee satisfaction. Staff hours and output data should be available on a daily basis. Labour rates are reviewed periodically. However employee satisfaction is probably best canvassed once or twice a year. I recommend that we conduct a weekly review of performance based on:

- Minutes per unit.

- Hours of overtime.

- Percentage of good output (or similar quality measure).

- Average hourly rate.

We should also commission a confidential employee satisfaction and involvement questionnaire.

BUDGET REVISION, VARIANCE ANALYSIS

85 ST DAVIDS

(a) **The material total variance**

This is the difference between what 1,000 units should have cost and what they did cost.

1,000 units should have cost (× £100)	£100,000
1,000 units did cost	£98,631
Material total variance	£1,369 F

The variance is **favourable** because the unit cost less than they should have cost.

Now, we can break down the material total variance into its two constituent parts: the material price variance and the material usage variance.

(b) **The material price variance**

This is the difference between what 11,700 kgs should have cost and what 11,700 kgs did cost.

11,700 kgs of Y should have cost (× £10)	£117,000
11,700 did cost	£98,631
Material Y price variance	£18,369 (F)

The variance is **favourable** because the material cost is less than it should have been.

(c)   The material usage variance

This is the difference between how many kilograms of Y should have been used to produce 1,000 units of X and how many kilograms were used, valued at the standard cost per kilogram.

1,000 units should have used (×10 kgs)	10,000 kgs
1,000 units did use	11,700 kgs
Usage variance, in kilograms	1,700 kgs (A)
	× £10
Usage variance in £	£17,000 A

The variance is **adverse** because more material was used than should have been used.

86   EASTER FUN

Raw material cost statement	£
Standard raw material cost of production	130,000
Variance (adverse shown as negative)	£ FAV/ – ADV
Material price	22,000
Material usage	−4,000
Material cost	18,000

Standard raw material cost of production

The standard Raw Material cost of production is the standard cost of actual production. In other terms, it is how much actual production should have cost, according to standards.

The 'Activity Data' table tells us that the standard cost of one item produced is $\dfrac{£126,000}{63,000 \text{ items}}$

That is £2 per item. Therefore, the actual production of 65,000 items should have cost 65,000 × £2 = £130,000.

Material price variance

Formula:	
Actual quantity purchased/used × Actual price	
V	
Actual quantity purchased/used × Standard price	
Then:	£
33,500 kgs	112,000
33,500 × £4.00	134,000
	———
Materials price variance	22,000 F

Alternative method

We could use what we call the **Did** and **Should** method to work out the answer.

33,500 kgs **did cost**	£112,000
33,500 kgs **should have cost** @ £4.00 per kg	**£134,000**
Variance	£22,000 F

The variance is **favourable** because the kilograms of material were cheaper than expected.

Material usage variance

> **Formula:**
> Actual quantity used × Standard price
> V
> Standard quantity used for actual production × Standard price
>
> | Then: | £ |
> |---|---|
> | 33,500 kgs × £4.00 | 134,000 |
> | 65,000 items × 0.5 kgs per item × £4.00 | 130,000 |
> | | _____ |
> | Materials usage variance | £4,000 A |

Alternative method

We could use what we call the **Did** and **Should** method to work out the answer.

65,000 items produced should have used 65,000 × 0.5 kgs per item	32,500 kgs
65,000 items did use	**33,500 kgs**
Variance	1,000 kgs A

1,000 kgs A × £4.00 = £4,000 Adverse variance.

The variance is **adverse** because we used more kilograms than expected.

87   ANNIVERSARY

Raw material cost statement	£
Standard raw material cost of production	12,500
Variance (adverse shown as negative)	£ FAV/ – ADV
Material price	–2,000
Material usage	–500
Material cost	–2,500

Standard raw material cost of production

The standard raw material cost of production is the standard cost of actual production. In other terms, it is how much actual production should have cost, according to standards.

The 'Activity Data' table tells us that the standard cost of one item produced is $\dfrac{£12,000}{1,200 \text{ items}}$

That is £10 per item. Therefore, the actual production of 1,250 items should have cost 1,250 × £10 = £12,500.

Material price variance

> **Formula:**
> Actual quantity purchased/used × Actual price
> V
> Actual quantity purchased/used × Standard price
>
> | Then: | £ |
> |---|---|
> | 1,300 kgs | 15,000 ⎫ |
> | 1,300 × £10.00 | 13,000 ⎭ |
> | | ‾‾‾‾‾‾ |
> | Materials price variance | 2,000 A |

Alternative method

We could use what we call the **Did** and **Should** method to work out the answer.

1,300 kgs **did cost**	£15,000
1,300 kgs **should have cost** @ £10.00 per kg	**£13,000**
Variance	£2,000 A

The variance is **adverse** because the kilograms of material were more expensive than expected.

Material usage variance

> **Formula:**
> Actual quantity used × Standard price
> V
> Standard quantity used for actual production × Standard price
>
> | Then: | £ |
> |---|---|
> | 1,300 kgs × £10.00 | 13,000 ⎫ |
> | 1,250 items × 1 kg per item × £10.00 | 12,500 ⎭ |
> | | ‾‾‾‾‾‾ |
> | Materials usage variance | £500 A |

Alternative method

We could use what we call the **Did** and **Should** method to work out the answer.

1,250 items produced should have used 1,250 × 1 kgs per item	1,250 kgs
1,250 items did use	**1,300 kgs**
Variance	50 kgs A

50 kgs A × £10.00 = £500 Adverse variance.

The variance is **adverse** because we used more kilograms than expected.

88   APPLES AND PEARS

Raw material cost statement	£
Standard raw material cost of production	68,460
Variance (adverse shown as negative)	£ FAV/ – ADV
Material price	–11,250
Material usage	–3,540
Material cost	–14,790

Standard raw material cost of production

The standard raw material cost of production is the standard cost of actual production. In other terms, it is how much actual production should have cost, according to standards.

The 'Activity Data' table tells us that the standard cost of one item produced $\dfrac{£65,520}{78,000 \text{ items}}$

That is £0.84 per item. Therefore, the actual production of 81,500 items should have cost 81,500 × £0.84 = £68,460.

Material price variance

> **Formula:**
> Actual quantity purchased/used × Actual price
> V
> Actual quantity purchased/used × Standard price
>
> | Then: | £ |
> |---|---|
> | 120,000 kgs | 83,250 ⎫ |
> | 120,000 × £0.60 | 72,000 ⎬ |
> | | ⎯⎯⎯ |
> | Materials price variance | 11,250 A |

Alternative method

We could use what we call the **Did** and **Should** method to work out the answer.

120,000 kgs **did cost**	83,200
120,000 kgs **should have cost** @ £0.60 per kg	**£72,000**
Variance	£11,250 A

The variance is **adverse** because the kilograms of material were more expensive than expected.

Material usage variance

Formula:
Actual quantity used × Standard price

V

Standard quantity used for actual production × Standard price

Then:	£
120,000 kgs × £0.60	72,000 ⎫
81,500 × 1.4 kg per item × £0.60	68,460 ⎬
	⎭
Materials usage variance	£3,540 A

Alternative method

We could use what we call the **Did** and **Should** method to work out the answer.

81,500 items produced should have used 81,500 × 1.4 kgs per item	114,100 kgs	
81,500 items did use	**120,000 kgs**	
Variance	5,900 kgs	A

5,900 kgs A × £0.60 = £3,540 Adverse variance.

The variance is **adverse** because we used more kilograms than expected.

89 INDEPENDENCE DAY

Raw material cost statement	£
Standard raw material cost of production	52,200
Variance (adverse shown as negative)	£ FAV/ – ADV
Material price	4,000
Material usage	–7,800
Material cost	–3,800

Standard raw material cost of production

The standard raw material cost of production is the standard cost of actual production. In other terms, it is how much actual production should have cost, according to standards.

The 'Activity Data' table tells us that the standard cost of one item produce $\dfrac{£50,400}{126,000 \text{ items}}$

That is £0.40 per item. Therefore, the actual production of 130,500 items should have cost 130,500 × £0.40 = £52,200.

Material price variance

> **Formula:**
>
> Actual quantity purchased/used × Actual price
>
> V
>
> Actual quantity purchased/used × Standard price
>
> | | £ |
> |---|---|
> | Then: | |
> | 120,000 kgs | 56,000 |
> | 120,000 × £0.50 | 60,000 |
> | | ——— |
> | Materials price variance | 4,000 F |

Alternative method

We could use what we call the **Did** and **Should** method to work out the answer.

120,000 kgs **did cost**	£56,000	
120,000 kgs **should have cost** @ £0.50 per kg	**£60,000**	
Variance	£4,000	F

The variance is **favourable** because the kilograms of material were less expensive than expected.

Material usage variance

> **Formula:**
>
> Actual quantity used × Standard price
>
> V
>
> Standard quantity used for actual production × Standard price
>
> | | £ |
> |---|---|
> | Then: | |
> | 120,000 kgs × £0.50 | 60,000 |
> | 130,500 items × 0.8 kg per item × £0.50 | 52,200 |
> | | ——— |
> | Materials usage variance | £7,800 A |

Alternative method

We could use what we call the **Did** and **Should** method to work out the answer.

130,500 items produced should have used 130,500 × 0.8 kgs per item	104,400 kgs	
130,500 items did use	**120,000 kgs**	
Variance	15,600 kgs	A

15,600 kgs A × £0.50 = £7,800 Adverse variance.

The variance is **adverse** because we used more kilograms than expected.

90 AUGUST

Raw material cost statement	£
Standard raw material cost of production	9,300
Variance (adverse shown as negative)	£ FAV/ – ADV
Material price	–210
Material usage	300
Material cost	90

Standard raw material cost of production

The standard raw material cost of production is the standard cost of actual production. In other terms, it is how much actual production should have cost, according to standards.

The 'Activity Data' table tells us that the standard cost of one item produced is $\dfrac{£9,000}{1,500 \text{ items}}$

That is £6.00 per item. Therefore, the actual production of 1,550 items should have cost 1,550 × £6.00 = £9,300.

Material price variance

> **Formula:**
>
> Actual quantity purchased/used × Actual price
>
> V
>
> Actual quantity purchased/used × Standard price
>
> | Then: | £ |
> |---|---|
> | 4,500 kgs | 9,210 ⎫ |
> | 4,500 × £2.00 | 9,000 ⎭ |
> | | |
> | Materials price variance | 210 A |

Alternative method

We could use what we call the **Did** and **Should** method to work out the answer.

4,500 kgs **did cost**	£9,210
4,500 kgs **should have cost** @ £2.00 per kg	**£9,000**
Variance	£210 A

The variance is **adverse** because the kilograms of material were more expensive than expected.

Material usage variance

Formula:

Actual quantity used × Standard price

V

Standard quantity used for actual production × Standard price

Then:	£
4,500 kgs × £2	9,000 ⎫
1,550 items × 3 kg per item × £2	9,300 ⎬
	———
Materials usage variance	£300 F

Alternative method

We could use what we call the **Did** and **Should** method to work out the answer.

1,550 items produced should have used 1,550 × 3 kgs per item	4,650 kgs	
1,550 items did use	**4,500 kgs**	
Variance	150 kgs	F

150 kgs F × £2.00 = £300 favourable variance.

The variance is **favourable** because we used fewer kilograms than expected.

91 BIRTHDAY

Direct labour cost statement	£
Standard direct labour cost of production	165,000
Variance (adverse shown as negative)	−3,000
Labour rate	−8,000
Labour efficiency	5,000
Labour cost	−3,000

Workings:

From the question, standard direct labour time per unit =

$$\frac{\text{Budgeted hours}}{\text{Budgeted number of items produced}}$$

Standard direct labour time per unit = $\dfrac{7,500 \text{ hours}}{10,000 \text{ units}}$

So standard direct labour time per unit = 0.75 hours, or 45 minutes.

We also need to work the standard direct labour cost per hour.

From the question, standard direct labour cost per hour = $\dfrac{\text{Budgeted cost in £}}{\text{Budgeted number of hours}}$

Therefore standard direct labour cost per hour = $\dfrac{£150,000}{7,500 \text{ hours}}$

Standard direct labour cost per hour = £20

Standard direct labour cost of production

11,000 units × 0.75 hrs × £20 per hour	£165,000
Actual cost of labour, as per question	£168,000
Variance	£3,000 A

Labour rate variance

> **Formula:**
>
> Actual labour hours paid × Actual rate
>
> V
>
> Actual labour hours paid × Standard rate
>
> | Then: | £ |
> |---|---|
> | 8,000 hours | 168,000 ⎫ |
> | 8,000 hours × £20 | 160,000 ⎭ |
> | | ——— |
> | Labour rate variance | 8,000 A |

Alternative method

We could use what we call the **Did** and **Should** method to work out the answer.

8,000 hours **did cost**	£168,000
8,000 hours **should have cost** @ £20 per hour	£160,000
Variance	£8,000 A

The variance is **favourable** because the average hourly rate was lower than expected.

Labour efficiency variance

> **Formula:**
>
> Actual hours worked × Standard rate
>
> V
>
> Standard hours worked for actual production × Standard rate
>
> | Then: | £ |
> |---|---|
> | 8,000 hours × £20 | 160,000 |
> | 11,000 units × 0.75 hours × £20 per hour | 165,000 |
> | | ——— |
> | Labour efficiency variance | £5,000 F |

We can use the **Did** and **Should** method to calculate the labour efficiency also.

11,000 units **did use**	8,000 hours
11,000 units **should have used** @ 0.75 hours per unit	8,250 hours
	250 hours
Multiplied by the standard (expected) rate	× £20 per hour
Variance is	£5,000

The variance is **favourable** because we used less direct labour than expected to make 11,000 units.

92   VALENTINE

Direct labour cost statement	£
Standard direct labour cost of production	589,000
Variance (adverse shown as negative)	−7,412
Labour rate	1,043
Labour efficiency	−8,455
Labour cost	−7,412

Workings:

From the question, standard direct labour time per unit =

$$\frac{\text{Budgeted hours}}{\text{Budgeted number of items produced}}$$

Standard direct labour time per unit = $\dfrac{64,500 \text{ hours}}{6,450 \text{ units}}$

So standard direct labour time per unit = 10 hours.

We also need to work the standard direct labour cost per hour.

From the question, standard direct labour cost per hour = $\dfrac{\text{Budgeted cost in £}}{\text{Budgeted number of hours}}$

Therefore standard direct labour cost per hour = $\dfrac{£612,750}{64,500 \text{ hours}}$

Standard direct labour cost per hour = £9.50

Standard direct labour cost of production	
6,200 units × 10 hours × £9.50 per hour	£589,000
Actual cost of labour, as per question	£596,412
Variance	**£7,412** A

Labour rate variance

Formula:	
Actual labour hours paid × Actual rate	
V	
Actual labour hours paid × Standard rate	
Then:	£
62,890 hours	596,412
62,890 hours × £9.50	597,455
	————
Labour rate variance	1,043 F

Alternative method

We could use what we call the **Did** and **Should** method to work out the answer.

62,890 hours **did cost**	£596,412
62,890 hours **should have cost** @ £9.50 per hour	**£597,455**
Variance	£1,043 F

The variance is **favourable** because the average hourly rate was lower than expected.

Labour efficiency variance

> **Formula:**
> Actual hours worked × Standard rate
> V
> Standard hours worked for actual production × Standard rate
>
> | Then: | £ |
> |---|---:|
> | 62,890 hours × £9.50 | 597,455 |
> | 6,200 units × 10 hours × £9.50 per hour | 589,000 |
> | | ———— |
> | Labour efficiency variance | £8,455 A |

We can use the **Did** and **Should** method to calculate the labour efficiency also.

6,200 units **did use**	62,890 hours
6,200 units **should have used** @ 10 hours per unit	**62,000 hours**
	890 hours
Multiplied by the standard (expected) rate	× £9.50 per hour
Variance is:	£8,455

The variance is **adverse** because we used more direct labour than expected to make 6,200 units.

MONTHLY OPERATING REPORTS, VARIANCE CALCULATIONS

93   OS

Monthly operating statement

Volume   72,000

	Flexed budget £	Actual £	Variance Fav/(Adv) £
Revenue	3,240,000	3,312,000	72,000
Costs			
Material	864,000	836,000	28,000
Labour	504,000	509,000	(5,000)
Distribution	18,000	19,500	(1,500)
Energy	205,000	201,250	3,750
Equipment hire (*)	40,000	42,000	(2,000)
Depreciation	212,000	206,000	6,000
Marketing	268,000	255,000	13,000
Administration	184,000	190,000	(6,000)
Total	2,295,000	2,258,750	36,250
Operating profit	945,000	1,053,250	108,250

(*) Note in stepped equipment hire costs

In the fixed budget, we have 76,000 units and equipment hire costs of £48,000. Each 'step' is made up of 15,000 units.

$$\frac{76,000 \text{ units}}{15,000 \text{ units}} = 5.06 \text{ steps, so 6 steps}$$

$$\frac{\text{Cost } £48,000}{6 \text{ steps}} = £8,000 \text{ per step}$$

In the **flexed** budget, we have 72,000 units.

$$\frac{72,000 \text{ units}}{15,000 \text{ units}} = 4.8 \text{ steps, so 5 steps}$$

5 × £8,000 = **£40,000** flexed equipment hire costs.

94 OS2

Monthly operating statement

Volume   80,000

	Flexed budget £	Actual £	Variance Fav/(Adv) £
Revenue	3,600,000	3,520,000	(80,000)
Costs			
Material	960,000	945,000	15,000
Labour	560,000	570,000	(10,000)
Distribution	20,000	19,500	500
Energy	225,000	219,250	5,750
Equipment hire	48,000	50,000	(2,000)
Depreciation	212,000	215,000	(3,000)
Marketing	268,000	253,000	15,000
Administration	184,000	166,000	18,000
Total	2,477,000	2,437,750	39,250
Operating profit	1,123,000	1,082,250	(40,750)

95 OS3

Monthly operating statement

Volume   110,000

	Flexed budget £	Actual £	Variance Fav/(Adv) £
Revenue	2,200,000	2,255,000	55,000
Costs			
Material	440,000	425,000	15,000
Labour	165,000	149,000	16,000
Distribution	11,000	12,500	(1,500)
Energy	106,000	110,250	(4,250)
Equipment hire	25,000	32,000	(7,000)
Depreciation	145,000	148,000	(3,000)
Marketing	260,000	255,000	5,000
Administration	172,000	181,000	(9,000)
Total	1,324,000	1,312,750	11,250
Operating profit	876,000	942,250	66,250

BACKWARDS VARIANCES CALCULATIONS

96   SALFORD

Tutorial note

Examiners believe that a good way to test understanding of a process is to give the candidate the end result, and ask them to find the input. If this involves variances, it is referred to as backwards variances.

Formula

Actual quantity purchased x Actual Price	
520 litres × £4.50	£2,340
V	
Actual Quantity purchased x standard price	
520 litres × ?	?
Materials price variance	£416 F

Actual quantity purchased x standard price must equal £2,340 + £416 = £2,756

The standard price per metre = £2,756/£520 litres = £5.30

97   WINNIFRED

Materials	£
Actual material cost	£ 18,980
Material price variance AQ × AP = 949 kgs × £20 = £18,980 AQ × SP = 949 kgs × £14 (W1) = £13,286	£ 5,694 A
Material usage variance AQ × SP = × £14 = £13,286 SQ × SP = 260 units × 5 kgs × £14 = £18,200	£ 4,914 F
Standard material cost of production	£ 18,200

Workings

If the standard cost per unit is £70 and each unit uses a standard quantity of 5 kgs, it means that each kg costs £14 (standard).

Section 3

MOCK ASSESSMENT QUESTIONS

TASK 1 (20 marks)

(a)   Match the data in the first column with the **appropriate source in the second column**.

Data	Source
Consumer price index (CPI) and other inflation data	Production Manager
Country-specific credit rating	Standard and Poor/Fitch/Moody agencies
Components prices for our star product	Operations Manager
Latest company customer service performance indicators	The World Bank
	The Office for National Statistics
	Suppliers and competitors

(b)   **As budget accountant, match each task with the person or group that you will need to contact:**

- You want confirmation that business operations are efficient in terms of using as little resources as needed, and effective in terms of meeting customer requirements.

- You are concerned about the number of complaints received from customers in the West Country.

- The materials usage budget needs a last minute update of wastage information.

Choose from:

- Regional Director

- Supervisor

- Operations Manager

- Management Accountant

(c)   **Take each item of cost in the list below and place it into its appropriate budget.**

Cost

Website development costs

Training to maintain and develop skills and capabilities

Kindergarten expenses for children of employees

Cost of conducting employee surveys

Cost of acquiring a property for investment purposes

Expected number of hours of idle time

Cleaning supplies

Public relations costs before product launch

Personnel

Cost of production

Maintenance

Capital expenditure

Marketing

(d) **Select an appropriate accounting treatment for each of the following costs:**

- Cost of hiring an additional supervisor in factory

- Raw material costs

- Cost of the cafeteria

- Admin salaries

- Computing services

- Production equipment maintenance

- Depreciation of machinery

- Redecoration of the top floor exhibition room

Options available are:

- Allocate to marketing overheads

- Allocate to administrative overheads

- Direct costs

- Charge to production in a machine hour overhead rate

- Charge to production in a labour hour overhead rate

- Activity based charge to production cost centres

(e) **Calculate the appropriate budgeted overhead recovery rate for the following production department.**

The department makes a variety of products and its annual budget for indirect costs is:

	£
Indirect labour	12,000
Supervisor wages	16,000
Depreciation of equipment	2,000
Machine maintenance	3,575
Canteen subsidy	3,425
Total	37,000

Note: The budget production of 37,000 units will require 44,400 machine hours and 18,500 direct labour hours.

Complete the following:

Overhead recovery should be based on labour hours/machine hours/units produced.

The recovery rate will be £_____ per _____.

TASK 2 (20 marks)

(a)   Complete the following production forecast for product P.

Units of product P

	Week 1	Week 2	Week 3	Week 4	Week 5
Opening stock	1,800				
Production					
Sub-total					
Sales	5,500	5,000	5,100	5,100	7,000
Closing stock					

Closing stock should be 22% of the following week's forecast sales.

(b)   The quarterly production requirements for product 'Zigma' are shown below.

7% of production fails the quality checks and must be scrapped.

How many items of product L must be manufactured to allow for waste?

	Month 1	Month 2	Month 3
Required units	99,000	100,000	101,000
Manufactured units			

(c)   Raw material purchases:

- 1,100 items of product X are to be manufactured in September.

- Each requires 7 metres of leather.

- 5% of raw material is wasted during manufacture.

- The opening stock will be 10,000 metres of leather.

- The closing stock will be 9,000 metres of leather.

How much material must be purchased?

Select from:

- 7, 000 m

- 7,700 m

- 7, 106 m

- 8, 106 m

(d)   Labour hours:

- 42,000 units of Company A's only product are to be manufactured in October

- Each one takes 19 minutes to produce

- 32 staff will each work 160 hours basic time

How many overtime hours must be worked to complete the production?

Select from:

- 5,120
- 8,080
- 8,180
- 13,300

(e) Department X manufactures three products, A, B and C.

Calculate the machine hours required to manufacture these in November.

Product	Units	Hours per unit	Hours required
A	120	1.8	
B	190	1.8	
C	190	3.0	
Total hours for Department X			

There are three machines in the department.

Each machine can be used for 260 hours in November. Additional machines can be hired if required.

How many additional machines should be hired? [   ]

TASK 3 (20 marks)

Operating budget

Enter the missing figures in the working schedules and operating budgets using the data from the production budget and the notes below.

Production budget	Units
Opening inventory of finished goods	90,000
Production	100,000
Sub-total	190,000
Sales	115,000
Closing inventory of finished goods	75,000

(a) **Complete these three working schedules.**

Materials

Each unit produced requires 0.5 kgs of material.

Closing inventory will be valued at the budgeted purchase price.

Materials	Kgs	£
Opening inventory	50,000	60,000
Purchases	44,000	77,000
Sub-total	94,000	137,000
Production		
Closing inventory of finished goods		

Labour

Each item takes 6 minutes to produce

26 staff work 210 basic hours each in the period.

Overtime is paid at 50% above the basic hourly rate.

Labour	Hours	£
Basic time at £12 per hour		
Overtime		
Total		

Overhead

Variable overhead is recovered on total labour hours

Overhead	Hours	£
Variable at £2.00 per hour		
Fixed		102,320
Total		

(b) **Now complete the operating budget.**

Closing Finished Goods Inventory will be valued at the budgeted production cost per unit.

Operating budget	Units	£ per unit	£
Sales revenue		2.35	
Cost of goods sold			£
Opening inventory of finished goods			150,000
Cost of production		£	
Materials			
Labour			
Overhead			
Closing inventory of finished goods			
Cost of goods sold			
Gross profit			
Overheads		£	
Administration		18,000	
Marketing		16,580	
Operating profit			

TASK 4 (20 marks)

(a) **Stratified sampling**

Calculate the number of customers to be interviewed from each age group to obtain a representative response from 201 interviews.

Age range	Up to 29	30 to 39	40 to 49	Over 49	Total
Number of customers	1,300	5,900	5,700	5,000	
Sample					

(b) **Break a budget down into accounting periods. Calculate the sales revenue and cost budgets for April using the budgeted unit data and information below.**

Each unit is made from 3 kgs of material costing £0.75 per kg.

It takes 5 minutes to make each item.

1,250 hours of basic time is available in the month. Any extra hours must be worked in overtime.

The basic rate is £16 per hour. Overtime is paid at 50% above basic rate.

Variable overhead relates to labour hours, including overtime.

Fixed production overhead costs are spread evenly through the year.

Budgeted units	Year	April
Units sold	209,000	18,200
Units produced	210,000	18,000
Budget in £	**Year**	**April**
Sales revenue	£1,149,500	
Material used	£472,500	
Direct labour	£300,000	
Variable production overhead	£77,000	
Fixed production overhead	£14,400	

(c) **Cash flow forecast**

Prepare the forecast from the operating budget and balance sheet assumptions. Enter receipts and payments as positive figures.

Balance sheet assumptions:

- Receivables will reduce by £2,500.
- Materials payables will increase by £2,500.
- Labour costs are paid in the period in which they are incurred.
- Other payables will reduce by £350.

Operating budget	£	£
Sales revenue		132,500
Expenditure		
Materials	32,250	
Labour	25,500	
Other costs	14,450	
		72,200
Operating profit		60,300

Cash-flow forecast	£	£
Sales receipts		
Payments		
Materials		
Labour		
Other costs		
Cash-flow forecast		

TASK 5 (20 marks)

La Mangerie runs a chain of restaurants in the North of England, and opened a new restaurant on 1 January in London – the first to be opened in the South of the country. Market research suggests that in London, the average selling price of a meal is £30 in similar restaurants.

You are aware of the following:

1   The London restaurant currently has 48 seats arranged in the same density as the other restaurants in the chain. In other similar London restaurants, tables tend to be higher density: the London restaurant could have an additional 12 tables if the existing tables were rearranged.

2   It has been observed that a number of the serving staff forget to offer customers the dessert menu, and often neglect customers towards the end of their meal.

3   A mystery diner (a customer who is employed by the company and visits the restaurant as an ordinary customer) has reviewed the restaurant and commented that the customer service was satisfactory, but not up the usual high standard. In particular, the serving staff were not very friendly and rarely smile.

The management accounts for the new London restaurant for the year ended 31 December 20X0, together with the average La Mangerie restaurant's management accounts for the same period, are shown below:

	London	Average
Number of meals served	14,892	19,710
Capacity of restaurant (maximum number of meals)	17,520	32,850
Average sales price per meal served	£22	£22
Number of main courses served	13,400	15,768
Percentage of customers who purchase a main meal	90%	80%
Number of deserts served	11,169	17,739
Percentage of customers who purchase a desert	75%	90%
Direct Labour cost per meal	£4	£2
Net profit margin	16%	31%
Utilisation of the restaurant (*)	85%	60%

(*) The utilisation of the restaurant is calculated as the number of meals served as a percentage of the capacity.

Write an email to the Managing Director in three parts:

(a)   comparing the London restaurant with the average restaurant and explaining the assumptions upon which your comparison is based.

(b)   suggesting other appropriate steps to improve the performance of the London restaurant.

(c)   explaining which of the planning assumptions are not totally within the delivery manager's control.

To	Managing Director	Date	(Today)
From	Budget Accountant	Subject	Review of indicators

(a)   Restaurant comparison

(b)   London – Performance Improvements

(c)   Controllability

TASK 6 (20 marks)

(a) Budget revision

You have submitted a draft operating budget to the budget committee. The committee has asked you to budget for an alternative scenario and calculate the increase or decrease in expected profit.

Complete the alternative scenario column in the operating budget table and calculate the increase or decrease in profit.

Assumptions in the first scenario

Material and labour costs are variable.

Depreciation is a stepped cost, increasing at every 12,000 units.

There is an allowance for an energy price rise of 8%.

Alternative scenario

Increase the selling price by 3%

Reduce the sales volume by 8%

Revise the energy price rise to 4%

Apart from the sales price per unit, do not enter decimals. Round to the nearest whole number, if necessary.

Operating budget	First draft	Alternative scenario
Sales price £ per unit	10.20	
Sales volume	60,000	
	£	£
Sales revenue	**612,000**	
Costs		
Material	135,000	
Labour	270,000	
Energy	108,000	
Depreciation	24,000	
Total	537,000	
Gross profit	75,000	
Increase/(decrease) in gross profit		

(b)   Variance analysis

Prepare the direct labour cost statement from the activity data provided.

Enter favourable variances as positive figures, for example 500.

Enter negative variances as negative figures, for example – 500.

Activity data	Items produced	Kgs used	Cost
Budget	3,000	4,500	9,000
Actual results	2,000	4,500	9,210

Raw material cost statement	£
Standard raw material cost of production	
Variance (adverse shown as negative)	
Material price	
Material usage	
Material cost	

TASK 7 (20 marks)

A monthly operating statement is shown below with some explanatory notes.

You are required to flex the budget, calculate variances and show whether each variance is favourable or adverse.

Monthly operating statement

	Budget	Actual
Volume	1,500	1,300
	£	£
Revenue	1,275,000	1,081,600
Costs		
Material	357,000	369,600
Labour	135,000	130,200
Distribution	6,300	7,000
Energy	5,300	5,300
Equipment hire	32,000	32,000
Depreciation	63,000	112,000
Marketing	231,000	235,000
Property expense	80,000	78,400
Total	909,600	969,500
Operating profit	365,400	112,100

Monthly operating statement

Volume   1,300

	Flexed Budget	Actual	Variance Fav/(Adv)
	£	£	£
Revenue		1,081,600	
Costs			
Material		369,600	
Labour		130,200	
Distribution		7,000	
Energy		5,300	
Equipment hire		32,000	
Depreciation		112,000	
Marketing		235,000	
Property expense		78,400	
Total		969,500	
Operating profit		112,100	

Enter adverse variances as minus

Notes:

- Material, labour and distribution costs are variable.

- The budget for energy is semi-variable. The variable element is £3.00 per unit.

- The budget for equipment hire is stepped, increasing at every 750 units of monthly production.

- Depreciation, marketing and administration costs are fixed.

TASK 8 (20 marks)

Exupery Ltd manufactures and sells leather jackets. The most popular pair of leather jackets produced is the 'Aviator' design and in May due to technical reasons this was the only leather jacket produced.

You work as an Accounting Technician at Exupery Ltd reporting to the Finance Director. Exupery operates a standard cost inventory system and all price variances are recorded on receipt of the purchase invoice. You are aware that the workers include new recruits to the company and they were recently taking 10% longer to produce each jacket than fully trained staff.

You have been presented with variances from the reconciliation statement shown below:

Reconciliation statement for Exupery Ltd – 4 Week period ending 31st May 20X6

Material A

Price	30,000 A
Usage	4,000 A

Material B

Price	2,950 A
Usage	750 A

Labour

Rate	480 A
Efficiency	2,400 A

Write an email to the Finance Director, in three parts, in which you explain:

(a) (i)   The possible causes of the material and labour variances detailed above;

(ii)   How important it is to investigate variances, whether adverse or favourable, and why.

(b)   How to set and manage a budget to drive improved performance.

(c)   How the introduction of standard costing could assist effective budgetary control.

| **To** | Finance Director | **Date** | (Today) |
| **From** | Accounting Technician | **Subject** | Review |

Section 4

MOCK ASSESSMENT ANSWERS

TASK 1

(a) Match the data in the first column with the appropriate source in the second column.

Data	Source
Consumer price index (CPI) and other inflation data	The Office for National Statistics
Country-specific credit rating	Standard and Poor/Fitch/Moody agencies
Components prices for our star product	Suppliers and competitors
Latest company customer service performance indicators	Operations Manager

(b) Who would you contact in each of the following situations?

- You want confirmation that business operations are efficient in terms of using as little resources as needed, and effective in terms of meeting customer requirements: **Operations Manager**.

- You are concerned about the number of complaints received from customers in the West Country: **Regional Director**.

- The materials usage budget needs a last minute update of wastage information: **Management Accountant**.

(c) Take each item of cost in the list below and place it into its appropriate budget.

Personnel

Training to maintain and develop skills and capabilities

Kindergarten expenses for children of employees

Cost of conducting employee surveys

Cost of production

Expected number of hours of idle time

Maintenance

Cleaning supplies

Capital expenditure

Cost of acquiring a property for investment purposes

Marketing

Website development costs

Public relations costs before product launch

(d)   **Select an appropriate accounting treatment for each of the following costs:**

- Cost of hiring an additional supervisor in factory: **Activity based charge to production cost centres**

- Raw material costs: **Direct costs**

- Cost of the cafeteria: **Activity based charge to production cost centres**

- Admin salaries: **Allocate to administrative overheads**

- Computing services: **Allocate to administrative overheads**

- Production equipment maintenance: **Charge to production in a machine hour overhead rate**

- Depreciation of machinery: **Charge to production in a machine hour overhead rate**

- Redecoration of the top floor exhibition room: **Allocate to marketing overheads**

(e)   **Calculate the appropriate budgeted overhead recovery rate for the following production department.**

The department makes a variety of products and its annual budget for indirect costs is:

	£
Indirect labour	12,000
Supervisor wages	16,000
Depreciation of equipment	2,000
Machine maintenance	3,575
Canteen subsidy	3,425
Total	37,000

Note: The budget production of 37,000 units will require 44,400 machine hours and 18,500 direct labour hours.

Overhead recovery should be based on **machine hours**.

The recovery rate will be £_____0.833_____ per _____machine hour_____.

TASK 2

(a)

	Week 1	Week 2	Week 3	Week 4	Week 5
Opening stock	1,800	1,100	1,122	1,122	1,540
Production	4,800	5,022	5,100	5,518	
Sub-total	6,600	6,122	6,222	6,640	
Sales	5,500	5,000	5,100	5,100	7,000
Closing stock	1,100	1,122	1,122	1,540	

(b)

	Month 1	Month 2	Month 3
Required units	99,000	100,000	101,000
Manufactured units	106,452	107,527	108,603

(c) 1,100 items × 7 metres of leather in total = 7,700 metres are needed for manufacture.

This needs grossing up for total number of metres to 7,700/0.95 = 8,106 metres.

Purchases = production requirements + Closing inventory 9,000 metres – opening inventory 10,000 metres.

Purchases = **7,106 metres**

(d) (42,000 units × 19 minutes) ÷ 60 = 13,300 hours needed.

32 staff × 160 hours = 5,120 hours available.

Therefore we need (13,300 – 5,120 hours) = 8,180 hours of overtime.

(e) Department X manufactures three products, A, B and C.

Calculate the machine hours required to manufacture these in November.

Product	Units	Hours per unit	Hours required
A	120	1.8	216
B	190	1.8	342
C	190	3.0	570
Total hours for department X			1,128

There are three machines in the department.

Each machine can be used for 260 hours in November. Additional machines can be hired if required.

How many additional machines should be hired?   2

Working:

1,128 hours required when (260 × 3) = 780 hours are available.

Therefore we need additional machines for 1,128 – 780 hours = 348 hours.

Therefore 2 additional machines are required.

TASK 3

(a) Materials

Materials	Kgs	£
Opening inventory	50,000	60,000
Purchases	44,000	77,000
Sub-total	94,000	137,000
Production	50,000	60,000
Closing inventory of finished goods	44,000	77,000

Labour

Labour	Hours	£
Basic time at £12 per hour	5,460	65,520
Overtime	4,540	81,720
Total	10,000	147,240

Overhead

Variable overhead is recovered on total labour hours

Overhead	Hours	£
Variable at £2.00 per hour	10,000	20,000
Fixed		102,320
Total		122,320

(b)

Operating budget	Units	£ per unit	£
Sales revenue	115,000	2.35	270,250
Cost of goods sold			£
Opening inventory of finished goods			150,000
Cost of production		£	
Materials		60,000	
Labour		147,240	
Overhead		122,320	329,560
Closing inventory of finished goods			247,170
Cost of goods sold			232,390
Gross profit			37,860
Overheads		£	
Administration		18,000	
Marketing		16,580	34,580
Operating profit			3,280

TASK 4

(a)

Age range	Up to 29	30 to 39	40 to 49	Over 49	Total
Number of customers	1,300	5,900	5,700	5,000	17,900
Sample	15	66	64	56	201

(b)

Budgeted units	Year	April
Units sold	209,000	18,200
Units produced	210,000	18,000
Budget in £	**Year**	**April**
Sales revenue	£1,149,500	£100,100 (W1)
Material used	£472,500	£40,500 (W2)
Direct labour	£300,000	£26,000 (W3)
Variable production overhead	£77,000	£6,600
Fixed production overhead	£14,400	£1,200

Workings:

(W1) In order to calculate the sales revenue in April, we need the budgeted selling price per unit. We can calculate this selling price as follows:

$$\text{Budgeted selling price per unit} = \frac{\text{Sales revenue for the year}}{\text{Number of units sold in the year}}$$

Tutorial note

Note that we are using the number of units sold here to calculate the April Sales Revenue. This is different from the rest of the question where we will use units produced to establish monthly costs.

$$\text{Budgeted selling price per unit} = \frac{£1,149,500}{209,000}$$

Budgeted selling price per unit = £5.50

Then, this budgeted selling price per unit of £5.50 applies to all the units sold in April, i.e. 18,200 units: 18,200 units × £5.50 = £100,100.

(W2) To calculate the cost of material used, we know from the question that *'each unit is made from 3 kgs of material costing £0.75 per kg.'*

We also know that in April we will produce 18,000 units.

Therefore, the material cost in April is equal to 18,000 units × 3 kgs × £0.75 = £40,500.

(W3) To calculate the cost of labour, we know from the question that it takes 5 minutes to make each item. Therefore in April, to make 18,000 items would take 18,000 × 5 minutes = 90,000 minutes.

$$\frac{90,000 \text{ minutes}}{60 \text{ minutes in an hour}} = 1,500 \text{ budgeted labour hours in April.}$$

Because only '*1,250 hours of basic time are available in the month*' and '*any extra hours must be worked in overtime*' (from the data in the question), it means that we will use up all the 1,250 basic hours and (1,500 − 1,250) = 250 hours of overtime will also be needed.

In summary, the 1,250 hours are paid £16 each, for a total of 1,250 × £16 = £20,000. We also need to pay overtime of 250 hours × £16 × 1.5 times = £6,000. So in total, direct labour cost for April will amount to £26,000.

(c)

Cash-flow forecast	£	£
Sales receipts		135,000 (W1)
Payments		
Materials	29,750 (W2)	
Labour	25,500 (W3)	
Other costs	14,800 (W4)	70,050 (W5)
Cash-flow forecast		64,950 (W6)

Workings:

(W1) Sales receipts will equal sales revenue, but we also need to take into account the movement in receivables. Here, our receivables have reduced by £2,500. This means that not only have we received the cash from our sales, but also reduced our receivables by £2,500 (i.e. they have paid £2,500 of their debt to us). Therefore, total cash received equals £132,500 + £2,500 = £135,000.

(W2) Materials payments will equal materials expenditure unless there is a movement in 'Materials payable', i.e. in the amount of money we owe to our creditors. Here, the 'materials payable' item increases by £2,500, which means we have a cash outflow for the expenditure of £32,250 **less** the £2,500 which increases our debt to creditors.

(W3) There is no delay in paying labour costs so the expenditure will equal the cash outflow.

(W4) Payments for other costs will equal expenditure unless there is a movement in 'Other payables', i.e. in the amount of money we owe to our creditors. Here, the 'Other payables' item decreases by £350, which means we have a cash outflow for the expenditure of £14,450 **plus** the £350 which decreases our debt to creditors.

(W5) Total expenditure = £29,750 + £25,500 + £14,800 = £70,050.

(W6) Cash flow forecast = £135,000 − £70,050 = £64,950.

KAPLAN PUBLISHING

TASK 5

To	Managing Director	**Date**	(Today)
From	Budget Accountant	**Subject**	Review of indicators

I attach the comparison between restaurants for your consideration and approval.

(a) Restaurant comparison

The purpose of this report is to compare the London restaurant and the average restaurant, and to suggest improvements in the second part.

The average price per meal served is the same at £22, the same as the average restaurant outside of the capital.

We also find that the London restaurant served a total of 13,400 main courses. This is less than the average restaurant out of London; however, it is a good result because it means that 90% of the London customers order a main course, compared to 80% in the average restaurant.

In London, the number of deserts ordered is also lower, in absolute terms and in percentage: only 75% of customers purchased desert. This could be explained by the staff not offering dessert or not providing customer service towards the end of the meal; it could also be linked to the friendliness (or lack of) of the staff.

The Net profit margin is almost half that of the average restaurant (16%). This could be because of London prices – the cost of rent and the manager's salary are probably higher due to the London location, and direct labour. The direct labour cost per meal is twice as high in London, due to wage costs being higher, as the capital is a costly place to live.

The utilisation of the restaurant is 85%, compared to the average of 60% which is very good and probably representative of the London market.

(b) London – Performance Improvements

The average price per meal is the same in and out of London, but we know that the average selling price of a meal in London is £30; Therefore, the London restaurant could put up its prices, in order to improve profits.

Furthermore, high direct labour rates also add weighting to the option to increase the price of the meal to £30.

The obvious action is, with regards to desert, to make sure that guests are attended to, and offered dessert. Simple customer feedback forms could be handed to customers and basic satisfaction ratings recorded in order to motivate staff and hopefully improve the number of customers ordering desert.

Increasing the number of tables would increase the capacity and probably increase the profit as the only additional costs would be some fixtures and fittings, additional labour costs and additional material costs. Additional contribution would probably be made.

The utilisation rates could be improved further by increasing the table density and thus the number of meals served.

(c) Controllability

Although the London restaurant manager should take ownership of its performance, there are aspects of it which are not wholly within his control. For example, the restaurant manager cannot control the economy and eating out is a discretionary expense that will be cut by diners in recessionary times.

TASK 6

(a)

Operating budget	First draft	Alternative scenario
Sales price £ per unit	10.20	10.506
Sales volume	60,000	55,200
	£	£
Sales revenue	**612,000**	**579,931**
Costs		
Material	135,000	124,200
Labour	270,000	248,400
Energy	108,000	104,000
Depreciation	24,000	24,000
Total	537,000	500,600
Gross profit	75,000	79,331
Increase/(decrease) in gross profit		4,331

(b)

Raw material cost statement	£
Standard raw material cost of production	6,000
Variance (adverse shown as negative)	£ fav/−adv
Material price	−210
Material usage	−3,000
Material cost	−3,210

TASK 7

Monthly operating statement

	Budget	Actual
Volume	1,500	1,300
	£	£
Revenue	1,275,000	1,081,600
Costs		
Material	357,000	369,600
Labour	135,000	130,200
Distribution	6,300	7,000
Energy	5,300	5,300
Equipment hire	32,000	32,000
Depreciation	63,000	112,000
Marketing	231,000	235,000
Property expense	80,000	78,400
Total	909,600	969,500
Operating profit	365,400	112,100

Monthly operating statement

Volume		1,300	
	Flexed Budget	Actual	Variance Fav/(Adv)
	£	£	£
Revenue	1,105,000	1,081,600	−23,400
Costs			
Material	309,400	369,600	−60,200
Labour	117,000	130,200	−13,200
Distribution	5,460	7,000	−1,540
Energy	4,700	5,300	−600
Equipment hire	32,000	32,000	−0
Depreciation	63,000	112,000	−49,000
Marketing	231,000	235,000	−4,000
Property expense	80,000	78,400	1,600
Total	842,560	969,500	−126,940
Operating profit	262,440	112,100	−150,340

Enter adverse variances as minus

TASK 8

To	Finance Director	**Date**	(Today)
From	Accounting Technician	**Subject**	Review

(a) **Variances – possible causes**

    (i)   I have reviewed the results for the period. Possible reasons for variances include:

Material price variance (adverse)

1   Market shortages pushing up prices

2   Using a different supplier – costing more

3   Standard doesn't anticipate price rises

4   Standard set when price index was lower

Material usage variance (adverse)

1   Sub-standard materials – excess waste

2   Measurement errors

3   Incorrect standard set

4   Mechanical breakdowns

5   Pilferage

6   Poorly trained new recruits using material inefficiently

Labour rate variance (adverse)

1   Incorrect standard set – overtime premiums not included

2   Failure to include future pay rises

3   Use of higher grade labour

4   Rush order necessitating overtime working

Labour efficiency variance (adverse)

1   Poorly trained recruits taking longer than fully trained staff

2   Poor quality material more difficult to process

    (ii)   Variance analysis is the evaluation of the differences between budgeted and actual results. This said it would be extremely important for the purposes of control to carry out this analysis on a regular basis.

           Both adverse and favourable variances should be analysed. This is due in part to the fact that there is a large inter-dependence between variances themselves. For example, the adverse materials usage variance and the adverse labour efficiency variance in Exupery could be linked: poor quality material generates more usage per unit, and can also contribute to lower efficiency if it causes machines to break down more often.

In instances where there is a favourable materials purchase price variance you might also have an adverse materials usage variance. This could be brought about by the fact that whilst the price may be cheaper the quality of the material may be less than expected leading to greater waste. It is particularly important where companies use responsibility accounting that production managers are not held accountable for variances caused by poor quality material.

In fact some if not all of the usage variance could be down to the purchased quality and is therefore the responsibility of the purchasing department.

Not all variances would be investigated all the time. Under normal circumstances you would expect to investigate the large variances (those above a certain amount or percentage). However, it should be noted that small variances happening frequently could be the signs of an increasing trend and should therefore not be ignored.

(b) To be challenging, budgets should be stretching and always strive for improvement. They also need to be achievable or will have an adverse effect on morale.

We can see from the operating statement that all variances are adverse. It can be argued that cost control is poor and that managers are not challenged to improve efficiency.

I recommend that we introduce stricter cost control all through the budget setting and implementation phases. Efficiency improvements need to be planned and introduced. A stretching budget is likely to motivate managers to improve performance. Variance need to be fully analysed and explained on a regular basis and corrective action taken promptly.

(c) Standard costing is an effective mechanism for bringing rigour to budgetary control. It makes sense to set standards for production resources at the level of a single unit of production. The standards can be multiplied by planned production levels to create cost budgets.

The system facilitates the calculation of detailed cost variances which helps managers to understand and manage the resources effectively.